Nowhere but *Up*

Nowhere but  Up

The Story of Justin Bieber's Mom

PATTIE MALLETTE

with A. J. Gregory

Revell

a division of Baker Publishing Group
Grand Rapids, Michigan

© 2012 by Life Projects, LLC

Published by Revell
a division of Baker Publishing Group
P.O. Box 6287, Grand Rapids, MI 49516-6287
www.revellbooks.com

Printed in the United States of America

Library of Congress Cataloging-in-Publication Data is on file at the Library of Congress, Washington, DC.

ISBN 978-0-8007-2189-3 (cloth)
ISBN 978-0-8007-2212-8 (intl. pbk.)

Unless otherwise indicated, Scripture quotations are from GOD'S WORD®. © 1995 God's Word to the Nations. Used by permission of Baker Publishing Group.

Scripture quotations labeled NIV are from the Holy Bible, New International Version®. NIV®. Copyright © 1973, 1978, 1984, 2011 by Biblica, Inc.™ Used by permission of Zondervan. All rights reserved worldwide. www.zondervan.com

Scripture quotations labeled NLT are from the Holy Bible, New Living Translation, copyright © 1996, 2004, 2007 by Tyndale House Foundation. Used by permission of Tyndale House Publishers, Inc., Carol Stream, Illinois 60188. All rights reserved.

Lyrics on pages 156–57 are from "Waves of Grace," written by David Noble. Copyright 1995. LITA Music (ASCAP). Administered by Justin Peters/Songs for the Planet, Inc., P.O. Box 40251, Nashville, TN 37204. International copyright secured. All rights reserved. Used by permission.

All dates, place names, titles, and events in this account are factual. The names of certain characters and some details have been changed in order to protect the privacy of those involved.

The internet addresses, email addresses, and phone numbers in this book are accurate at the time of publication. They are provided as a resource. Baker Publishing Group does not endorse them or vouch for their content or permanence.

Life Projects is represented by Fedd & Company, Inc.

12 13 14 15 16 17 18   7 6 5 4 3 2 1

To my heavenly Father,
for being the ultimate Redeemer

Foreword

by Justin Bieber

My mom is the strongest woman I've ever met. I've always known it, but this book has helped to remind me just how strong she is. I've always admired her. She is an example of a person who doesn't compromise and doesn't quit. Just by who she is, my mom inspires me to be a good man. And she is always pushing me to be better.

I know she has given up a lot and made a ton of sacrifices to be my mother and raise me. And I'm excited to see new things, like this book, unfold in her own life. I might be biased as her son and her biggest fan, but I'm a strong believer that my mom's story is one that needs to be heard. As you read this book, you'll find that her life wasn't easy, as much of her early years were a struggle. It was hard to read about my mom's pain, but I recognize how important it is for her story to be told.

Many women who have gone through similar experiences need a little bit of hope—to know there is light at the end of the tunnel. That's what I know my mom can give through this story. As she shares about finding strength and peace, I hope you find the same. I wish you the best in your own journey. Know that God is with you.

I love you, Mom.

A Note from the Author

Thank you for reading my story. Before you dive in, I'd like to share with you my heart and my vision for this book. It's about more than simply me telling about my life, because frankly, there are many parts of my story that I'd rather forget and that I'm certainly not proud of. But there are also instances of amazing grace for which I'm supremely thankful. I decided to tell my story not only for my own healing from a difficult past but also to help bring healing and liberation to those of you who may have suffered in similar ways. A major key in my healing was finding my voice—the voice I never had as a little girl. By giving that little girl a voice, I hope to help others find theirs and find the courage to use it. My heart's desire is that my words bring others the hope that I have discovered in my own life.

I write especially for those of you who know the pain of sexual abuse as well as all those who have experienced abandonment, rejection, and fear. I write for those of you who believe you are damaged goods and who identify yourselves by the wounds of your past. I write to encourage you that there is hope, there is light, and there is a life worth living beyond the pains of the past. I write because I believe with my whole heart that you—just like me—can find your way to ultimate healing and freedom.

I understand that being honest carries some risk. The world is full of critics. Sharing bits and pieces of my life, and particularly of truth that isn't very pretty and at times is hard to read, may lead to some questions about my intentions. My intentions with this book are not to accuse, vilify, or point fingers at anyone. I do not wish to share my story at the expense of hurting others. Believe me, I've made my share of mistakes, some of which I tell about in this book.

I have wrestled long and hard with how to authentically write about the painful details of my life without casting a shadow on the people I love most. I ask that you read this book without throwing stones. We're all human and we've all made mistakes. Most of us, however, don't have them aired out for the world to read. Understand that people change, as I have, and everyone deserves grace and a second chance. There are two sides to every story. This book is my side.

I'd like to acknowledge my family and Jeremy for their understanding in how they, and especially some of their vulnerable moments, appear as part of this book. They are part of a bigger picture. Their experiences too can help others for a greater purpose. I honor them for their courage and commend them for their bravery as I recount some hurtful memories.

You'll see that Jeremy and I had a particularly difficult relationship. We were both young and immature when we were together. And I especially want you to know that just as I have changed, Jeremy has too, and he is a different man than he once was. I'm proud of how far he has come as a man and as a father. Today, I consider him a friend.

I'm grateful to all the family members and friends who are part of my story. I love them with all my heart and am thankful beyond words.

One

I spent years wrestling with darkness and drowning in torment. And I've spent most of my adult life sifting through the tangled web of emotional wounds and the debris left by the darkness in my childhood. I've hobbled back to the early years of my life, painfully resting at the different events that shaped me through my childhood. And I've learned that sometimes you have to go through your past to get to your future.

One night I had a dream in which my job was to clean out every room in a gigantic house, which was made up mostly of bedrooms. The bedrooms belonged to girls of different ages, from babies to teenagers, and were stuffed with clothes, garbage, and toys piled almost a foot high. I was so overwhelmed by the task. In the first room, I couldn't do much more than clear a bit of space around my feet by shoving some of the stuff to the side. So I decided to go to another room and try again. It was more of the same. I repeated this process in room after room, with the same result—all I could manage to do was clear a small space around my feet. I was frustrated. I didn't have a clue how to start cleaning up.

As I stood there, unable to move, I heard a voice. Instinctively, I knew it belonged to God. "Go to the beginning of the house," He said.

My dream self knew what I had to do. I went to the first room of the house, the living room, and started removing every single object from the room. I dumped everything outside—couches, lamps, rugs, tables, pictures, books—until the room was empty. Then I scrubbed the walls clean, repainted them, and brought back in only the items I wanted. One room was clean. Now I knew how to go back and clean the rest.

When I woke from the dream and meditated on it, I saw a correlation between the house in that dream and the events of my childhood. The different rooms represented me at different ages and the areas of my life I was trying to clean up or heal as an adult. The simple instruction from the dream struck me.

Go to the beginning.

I had already explored the early years of my childhood in therapy, and though the thought sounded crazy, I wondered if the dream meant I needed to revisit my life before I was born. Maybe some trauma had taken place while I was still in my mother's womb. I felt stupid for even entertaining the idea. Go back to the womb? What sense does that make? How could something you never knew about have such a traumatic effect on you later in life? But I was willing to do it. I was desperate.

My father was an alcoholic who followed in the footsteps of his alcoholic father. I don't know much about my dad because he left when I was two years old. I do know he was violent. My dad even pushed my mom around when she was pregnant with me. I've learned from talking to other family members that my dad was like a chameleon.

While others saw him as a loving, charming, and gentle husband and father, we saw his hidden dark side.

Knowing I experienced violence even before I made it out into the real world disturbs me. It makes me think I showed up instantly unwanted. I mean, seriously, what kind of warm welcome can await a baby coming into a family filled with physical abuse? It seems my future was marred from the start.

My mom, Diane, was the oldest of ten children. She met my dad and got pregnant when she was sixteen, and they started a new life together in the city of Timmins, Ontario, Canada, before eventually moving to Stratford, a ten-hour drive away.

My brother, Chris, was born in 1967, followed just eighteen months later by Sally, the sister I never met. When Sally was five years old, her life was tragically cut short. My mom was four months pregnant with me.

I'm told it was a chilly November morning when my brother and Sally were getting ready to walk across the street to the baby-sitter's house. As the sun made its early climb, Chris and Sally walked hand-in-hand toward the curb. Maybe Sally wanted to walk faster. Maybe she didn't feel like holding her brother's hand. No one knows why, but she let go. In the time it takes to blink, Sally had unlocked her little fingers from Chris's strong grip and raced into the street, leaving a trail of giggles echoing behind. She didn't see the oncoming car. Chris did. He cried out, but it was too late. Sally died upon impact.

I can't imagine the guilt my brother must have felt after watching the car slam into his sister's tiny body, knowing his best attempt to save her couldn't cheat death. Chris and I only ever spoke of the accident one time. I'm sure the devastation was too much for him to revisit again and again. Just as it was for my mom.

My heart breaks when I think about the agonizing grief my mom went through, the pain that never goes away when you lose a child. And to endure the loss while pregnant? How do you mourn one child while carrying another in your womb? Is it even possible to grieve and celebrate at the same time?

Of course, I never knew any of this until much later. My mother never spoke about Sally's death. In fact, I didn't even know I had a sister until I was around ten years old when this time, I was the one who was hit by a car.

I was riding my bike down the street on a sweltering summer day, not paying much attention to my surroundings. Without looking, I swerved to cross the street and didn't see the car coming from behind. It slammed into me, knocking me off the bike and onto the concrete road.

I wasn't hurt, but my mom and brother saw the accident and started screaming and crying. They made a huge scene and dragged me, sporting only minor scrapes and bruises, into the house. I was both puzzled and annoyed by the drama. "What is going on?" I demanded.

Mom and Chris finally calmed down enough to talk without the hysterics. They asked if I remembered the pictures of the little girl we had around the house a long time ago. I didn't remember. Or maybe I thought they were pictures of me so I hadn't paid much attention.

My mom said, "They were of your sister, Sally. She got hit by a car and died when she was five." I felt like I was in a *Twilight Zone* episode. I had a sister? Who was dead? It was all very strange. Then my memory pushed a tiny space through the fog and I remembered. I remembered pictures of Sally in the photo albums—pictures my mom had told me were of me. My sister and I looked practically identical. I imagine there were times my mom looked at me and saw a ghost, a phantom of my big sister.

Later I wondered if Sally's death had anything to do with the disconnect I always felt between me and my mother. For years this disconnect had me convinced I was adopted, because I always felt like I didn't belong.

Every now and then something would drive that powerful feeling to the surface and I'd go on a rampage. I remember one time in my teens when I frantically searched the house for a piece of evidence— anything that would confirm I was adopted. I had convinced myself my birth mother was somewhere out there. Maybe she was even looking for me.

I threw open every cupboard in the kitchen, rattling the glasses and china like an aftershock. I opened and slammed shut desk and dresser drawers throughout the house. There had to be something somewhere. Just one measly document. I rummaged through closets, tossing aside old shoes, musty sweaters, and dusty boxes of God-knows-what. I turned the house upside down that day like a narc looking for drugs.

With an unexplained desperation, I finally cried to my mom, "I know I'm adopted! Stop lying to me. Just tell me where the papers are. I know it's true."

My mom must have thought I was nuts. "Stop it," she begged. "What are you talking about?" She grabbed a pair of photos and shoved them in my face, comparing our baby pictures side by side. "You look just like me! Why would you even think you're adopted?"

But I couldn't stop thinking about it. And I couldn't calm down. Something in me was still convinced I didn't belong. This was not my home. She was not my mother.

Where did those suspicions come from? And why did they affect me on such a deep level?

Go back to the beginning.

Damaging feelings don't just show up out of nowhere. They're birthed from experiences, from moments that wield the power to shape us. Sometimes we can't even recognize the magnitude of those pivotal events until years later.

When my dad left us, it ripped a hole in my heart—one that began filling with thoughts and feelings that would challenge and ultimately damage my identity and self-worth. The wound of being abandoned travels deep and forever changes you.

Even today I can still close my eyes and feel the emotional chaos that marked my heart when he walked out. I was only two when my dad left, but I still remember it vividly, as if it happened yesterday. In fact, it's my earliest childhood memory.

I remember my brother and me standing by the front door, blinking our big eyes and looking up to our father as he pulled on his jacket. *He looks so serious. Where's he going? Why is he taking a big suitcase? Mommy?* As my dad knelt down before the two of us, he handed me a parting gift, a Thumbelina doll. When I touched her plastic skin and looked into her big eyes that stared back at mine, I decided she was my best friend. As long as I had her, she never left my side.

"I love you so much," Daddy began. "But I have to move far away." He hugged each of us and slowly stood up, looking like a looming giant next to the toddler me. "I'll always love you."

As he turned his back to me, I could see his big hand pause on the knob of the front door. It felt like an eternity passed before he finally twisted the knob, opened the door, and walked out of our apartment. As the door slowly closed behind him, my heart reached out. I was too confused to actually cry out, but on the inside I was screaming for my dad. *Don't leave! Come back. Please, I need you.* But it was too late. Daddy was gone. It would be the last time I would see him until I was nine years old.

As an adult, I've grieved not having had my dad around to call me princess, to tell me how beautiful I was, and to threaten the boys I dated. I've mourned the loss of not having a dad I could curl up and feel secure with. A dad who would teach me how to be a self-respecting woman. A dad who would remind me that I was valued and worth more than perhaps I believed I was.

In that moment when I was two years old, though, all I wanted so desperately was to climb into my mother's arms and be soothed by the tenderness only a mother could give. But I couldn't. The day my dad left was the day I had to start growing up. I had to wipe my own tears and pull myself up by the bootstraps. There was no time for sadness. No room for confusion.

It was also the day I began to learn that my mother, who did an excellent job working hard to provide for and care for our physical needs, wasn't going to offer me the kind of warm and fuzzy maternal affection or the words of affirmation I longed for. She couldn't.

She had her own burdens to contend with. Her life in an abusive relationship, the grief of losing a daughter, and the added stress of her husband leaving her to be solely responsible for caring for two children stripped her of the ability to offer the kind of emotional support I needed. My mother was and still is a very strong woman. I, however, didn't have that kind of steel survival strength. Not yet.

Mom remarried when I was six, and I thought I had found my golden ticket. Bruce Dale was quiet, good-natured, and every bit in love with my mother. They were head over heels for each other, stealing kisses every chance they got. When Mom and Bruce were first together, he and I would watch boxing on TV. I'd climb on his lap, unable to take my eyes off of the sweaty boxers exchanging crushing blows, and proudly tell him, "I'm gonna be a boxer one day!" I loved the thought of Bruce becoming my daddy.

Bruce brought with him two children of his own, Candie, thirteen, and Chuck, eleven. Candie was a sweetheart and I looked up to her. She was a good big sister and always made time for me and made me feel special. My stepbrother had a gentle nature like his father, and he was fun to be around. I loved them both.

The more I got to know Bruce, the more I liked him. Especially because I knew how well he treated my mother. On August 15, 1981, the day of their wedding, I was so excited I could hardly stand it. My mom looked so pretty with her short hair brushed in a soft wave to the side. She wore a turquoise chiffon dress that complemented her eyes and held a small bouquet of beautiful white and pink roses. Bruce stood tall and proud next to her. He looked sharp in his dark brown suit. Even the tufts of hair that normally jutted out from his almost-bald head were neatly combed down. The boys wore light corduroy jackets with their butterfly-collared shirts sticking out like sore thumbs. They looked uncomfortable in their fancy clothes, like they wanted to tear them off and throw on some jeans. Candie and I wore pretty white dresses and matching knee-high socks. I got my hair done and even used hairspray for the first time.

But for me, the wedding was about more than having to look sharp. This was my moment. I would have a new dad. A dad who loved me. A dad who wanted to stay. I thought this was the best thing that could ever happen to me.

Later that evening, I called out for my new dad, who was in the other room. "Daddy," I said. I'd had such a deep longing to say that word. I wanted it in my vocabulary permanently. I wanted it to stay there so I could rest in the assurance that I had a daddy. That he would love and protect me. That he wasn't going anywhere.

Daddy. That was all I had ever wanted.

But at that simple two-syllable word from my lips, my brother Chris exploded.

Chris pulled me close to him so Bruce couldn't hear what he was about to say. "That is not your dad," he hissed in my face. "That is your mother's husband. He is a stranger in this house. Do not call him Daddy. You already have a dad!"

And after that, I never did. I've always liked Bruce, but I also looked up to Chris. After all, he was my older brother, so I respected his wishes. But in the process, I missed out on what could have been such a special relationship with my stepdad.

In Chris's defense, I can understand now where he was coming from then. He was seven years older than me, so he'd had more time with our dad than I had. Naturally, he felt more of an attachment with his father than I did. And having been the only male in our house for a few years, he may have felt threatened by the new male figure in our home. I don't believe for a second Chris knew how deeply wounding his words were. I'm sure that had he known, he wouldn't have said them.

On that day, though, I immediately created a distance between my stepdad and me. For the rest of my childhood, he would never take on the role of a father, because I never even gave him a chance. Before Bruce had the opportunity to be a true father figure, I had already shut him down. He never did anything wrong or hurtful, but in my eyes he would always be my mother's husband. Not my dad. I kept him at a safe distance back then, at arm's length.

As distant as I was from my mom and Bruce growing up, I was also distant from religion. My siblings and I grew up as nonpracticing Catholics. We never went to mass. Sundays weren't reserved for church. They were reserved as a day of R and R for my mom and Bruce. They both worked hard at their blue-collar jobs during the week, and come Sunday, it was time for them to unwind. Catch a game on TV. Do some shopping. Visit family. Maybe even go out for a big breakfast.

Around the time my mom remarried, my neighborhood friend, Robbie Wigan, invited me to church one week. My mom and Bruce didn't mind. It gave me something to do. While my mom shuffled around our modest kitchen half asleep, ripping open a package of filters to start the morning pot of coffee, I was upstairs finding something nice to wear. A pretty dress. Shiny shoes.

After I finished getting ready, I bounced down the stairs, yelled "Bye!" to my parents, and skipped four houses down to Robbie's house. I piled into the Wigans' station wagon with my little buddy and his family. I was so excited about going to church. I wasn't quite sure what I was excited for—I mean, who associates the word *excited* with church?—but it felt like an adventure.

As we made our way to the service, the adults in the front seat chatted away about boring grownup stuff as a tape of easy listening music played. Robbie and I gabbed away about little kid things.

Sunday school was a whirlwind of stories, crayons, crafts, songs, and snacks. I sat next to Robbie, utterly mesmerized. I was entranced by the fun and by the other kids who laughed and drew colorful pictures of Jesus. They all seemed happy to be there. Church wasn't a drag, a boring chore like washing the dishes or cleaning your room. Church was, well, fun. I liked this kind of fun. This was fun that I wanted. I wondered why my family never went to church.

When class was almost over, the sweet teacher with the big hair asked if I wanted to accept Jesus into my heart. Well, of course! Why wouldn't I? From what I could tell from the Bible stories and the cool-looking pictures, I liked Jesus. I wanted Him to be my friend. And I was even more tickled to hear that Jesus was waiting to be my friend first. Imagine that! So I accepted Jesus into my heart as a Sunday school teacher nodded approvingly beside a flannel board of colorful felt Bible characters.

I believe God had a hook in my life from that moment on. But even though I opened the door, I was only five years old. A lot of life was waiting to happen. And even though I believe my early exposure to God planted a seed for my future, faith wasn't going to keep bad things away. It wouldn't shield me when I was robbed of my innocence. Again and again.

Two

To look at our family, we were normal—whatever "normal" means (it means something different to everyone). My childhood appeared to be rather uneventful. Our small two-story house was nestled in a quiet suburban neighborhood in Stratford, Ontario, Canada. My mom and stepdad worked hard at their blue-collar jobs to provide for our family. Our block was home to kids of all ages, and we played together all the time.

Just about every day someone knocked at my front door to ask if I could come out and play or if they could come in and play with me at my house. Didn't have to ask me twice. My friends and I rode bikes. We hung out at the jungle gym of the elementary school just down the block. I went over to my friends' houses and we ate homemade chocolate chip cookies while making Lite-Brite art, playing with fruity-scented Strawberry Shortcake dolls, or trying to figure out the Rubik's

Cube. My friend Robbie and I organized block parades with the kids in the neighborhood. We even put on plays with the other kids when we were older. We'd write our own scripts, sell tickets door-to-door, and perform on a makeshift stage I owned.

I had birthday parties with loads of colorful balloons and presents, and I'd always invite all the kids from the neighborhood. I played with Cabbage Patch Kids and stuffed animals. I had stupid elementary school crushes on boys. When it snowed in the winter (and it snowed a lot), my siblings and I made snowmen and forts. We took family vacations on occasion; we even went to Florida one year. We hosted our extended family for Thanksgiving and stuffed ourselves with delicious food. We decorated the tree for Christmas and battled the malls for presents.

On the outside, our life was normal. Nothing out of the ordinary. Nothing unusual. Nothing suspect. But underneath all the apparent normalcy, I was enduring many years of sexual abuse.

My earliest sexual memory is of what started out as an innocent game of doctor, minus the stethoscope and medicine bag. As with many of the other incidents, I can recapture only blurry details, as if the incident happened in a fog. But even in light of the fuzzy remembering, the memories are still there.

I remember lying on a table. I was about three years old. Older kids were present, familiar faces. Anxiety filled the air, like a dark secret was about to be exposed. I was playing the role of a patient, expecting the "doctor" to diagnose some scary disease. Someone held a thermometer, I assumed to check how high my pretend fever was.

I wasn't prepared for what came next. The thermometer was inserted in places in my body where it didn't belong. I remember feeling gross. It felt wrong. Strangely, though I don't have any specific memories of incidents prior to this time, I remember feeling like it had happened before. Like I had been touched in a similar way at another time. I don't know for sure about that. What I do know is that it would not be the last time.

22

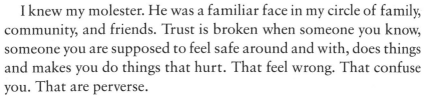

I knew my molester. He was a familiar face in my circle of family, community, and friends. Trust is broken when someone you know, someone you are supposed to feel safe around and with, does things and makes you do things that hurt. That feel wrong. That confuse you. That are perverse.

I was five years old. I was carefully choosing the prettiest crayons to use on the next page of my coloring book when he walked into the room where I played. He wasn't wearing any clothes. The crayon that was just about to shade a colorless sun a warm yellow slipped through my hands and fell to the floor with an echoing thud. I was confused and scared. I was shocked.

Why is he naked? Why is he showing me his private parts?

I don't know how I was directed to or what happened after it was over, but I ended up touching him. I didn't want to; I just followed his lead. I did as I was told. Just like a good little girl.

For the next five years, his inappropriate touching continued. And for the next five years, I kept quiet, confused by the physical attention. I was confused by the way he would caress my skin, the parts of my body that were always covered in public for a reason—they were private.

Unfortunately, he wasn't my only molester. During the same time period a second molester entered my life. Another person I knew. Another person I trusted.

I remember his hands reaching out to pull down my underwear. My body stiffened. I had no defense. I was helpless. *Again? Oh, God. Why me?*

Other times we were in a quiet room. Though we were behind closed doors, at times we were only a few feet away from adults. Adults who could have been watching TV. Or eating. Or talking on the phone. Or cleaning up. Or reading the paper. Adults doing normal, everyday things. I could hear doors open and slam shut. I could hear footsteps. I could hear talking. I sometimes heard people nearby, people I hoped would rescue me or would care enough to even notice something bad was happening close by. But no one did.

The abandonment that overwhelmed my heart as a little girl who watched her daddy walk away was quickly morphing into something bigger than me. I couldn't see it at the time, but hindsight, as we know, is always 20/20. As I look back, I can see a child who felt sad. Unwanted. Unloved. Unlovable. Those feelings grew like a fungus and made me hungry for attention.

I knew the sexual touch was wrong, but in a warped way I didn't mind so much. Don't misunderstand me—I didn't *like* what was happening. But I wanted so desperately to find and grab hold of a sense of being loved and wanted. No matter what it looked like, no matter where it came from.

I was sexually violated so many times that as the years went by it began to feel normal. It's a strange marriage—knowing something is wrong yet at the same time finding it familiar and commonplace. By the time I was in my mid teens, I was sick of asking the same questions over and over again: *What's wrong with me? What am I doing to attract sexual attention? Why am I such a magnet for abuse?*

Maybe it was that obvious. Maybe, just maybe, I thought, I was made for sex. Maybe I was just a dirty girl. At one point I even toyed around with the idea of becoming a prostitute or a stripper. It seemed to fit the mold my life was creating for me.

You can't help thinking these crazy things when sexual abuse rears its ugly head time and time again. It's like a Whac-A-Mole game. No matter how hard you hit it to keep it down, the mole keeps popping up. My life was littered with perversions from so many different kinds of abusers—young and old, male and female, familiar faces and those I barely knew.

When I think about some of the events today, it's like an explosion goes off and I see one moment frozen in time. One scene. One foggy face. I know what's happening, but I don't see intricate detail. I've learned that's normal. Like most victims of sexual abuse, I had to forget some parts of the events in order to survive. It's a defense mechanism. My mind wouldn't allow me to remember the play-by-play because I couldn't handle it. Most people can't.

But some things are impossible to forget.

Sometimes when I close my eyes, I can see a girl from school. She is trying to teach me about pleasure. A pleasure that doesn't come from dolls and roller skates and hugs from Grandma. A pleasure I don't understand. She is showing me things about my body beyond my level of maturity. I can barely master writing a full sentence, but I know how to make myself feel good.

I close my eyes and I can see a neighborhood girl coming over to play. We had a gigantic plastic car in our backyard, probably belonging to Chris or Chuck. We're making up stories about going on a long drive into the sunset with our Prince Charming. Then the mood shifts, and she is taking our little kid fun to an adult level. A level that makes me feel uncomfortable and dirty.

After she finishes, I feel guilty. I think about church. About how I asked Jesus to come into my heart. I am ashamed. What have I done? God must be disappointed. Maybe He even hates me. The worry is crushing. I tell this girl, "I don't want to do this. God can see us. He knows what we're doing. And it's wrong."

My protests fall on deaf ears. She rolls her eyes and reassures me. "Pattie, God's too busy to be bothered by us." I don't know why her reply makes sense to me, but it does. It's a convenient justification to excuse what was being done to me. And it seems about right. I do what many of us do—I compare my heavenly Father to my earthly father. If my dad doesn't care about me, why should God? If my daddy is too busy for me, why should God be interested in my life or what I am doing?

And then there was a babysitter when I was ten. He was only a few years older than me. As we sat in front of the TV watching ALF, the furry little alien guy who had a knack for annoying the heck out of Willie Tanner, the babysitter asked if I could model for him. My eyes lit up. Model? Of course! I was a theatrical nut, born to sing, dance, and act. Walking down a pretend runway and wearing pretend designer duds sounded like fun.

But he wasn't interested in the funky outfits I would choose. Or my dramatic catwalk. Or the bright red, supermodel-worthy lipstick I would put on. It was my body he wanted to look at.

The first time I took off to the bedroom to change out of my clothes, he stopped me. With a wide grin he said, "Don't change in there. Bring your clothes out in the living room." He pointed directly to the empty space in front of him. "Change right here."

He immediately saw the confused look on my face and dove into some serious persuading. He managed to convince me I would be safe with him, that because he was trusted enough to watch me, he could be trusted to see me take my clothes off. "No big deal," he assured me.

On one hand, I felt disturbed. On the other hand, I was so used to being objectified that I didn't give it much thought. Being naked and being touched in private places was my normal, so the babysitter's request was familiar territory to me.

By the time most kids are speeding down the street on a bike with training wheels, the doors of sexuality were swung wide open in my life, revealing to me a world full of shame, manipulation, and selfish desire. A world I didn't know how to escape. Sex followed me, lurking in dark corners waiting for the perfect ambush. My longing to be loved made me easy prey.

The repeated cycle of abuse awakened sexual desires way too early for me. It created in me an immature curiosity I didn't quite understand or know what to do with. I was still a kid, after all. And kids don't need to be touched in private places on their body. Kids don't need to be touching adults in private places on their body. Kids don't need to be experimenting with parts of their body they have no maturity level to understand. Kids need to bask in their innocence, play outside, and go on carefree adventures around the neighborhood, not spend their lives conflicted by acts that bring shame, confusion, and guilt.

But that's not how it was for me.

I'm not sure how old I was when I found the stack of dirty magazines at the bottom of a nightstand. I flipped through them. I saw the explicit images, and like seeing a car accident on the side of the road, I stopped and stared. I wasn't sure what was going on in the pictures, but I couldn't take my eyes off of them.

Just like the time I caught a glimpse of a porn channel on TV. I had trouble sleeping one night, and instead of tossing and turning, I went downstairs to get a glass of water. I never made it to the kitchen. From the top of the hallway staircase, I could see the television in the living room. My eyes were glued to the screen as I was faced with the unforgettable image of naked people performing sexual acts.

My foot rested on a creaky floorboard and gave me away. In a heartbeat, I was met with an angry "Patricia! Get back to bed!" I was so startled I ran like a bat out of hell, my face flushed with embarrassment. I wasn't sure why I'd been yelled at so harshly, but I felt deeply ashamed. What I saw on the screen stayed with me for years. And when I got older and my parents went out for the night, I tried to search for those same movies.

Let me be clear—I know my parents never intended for me to ever catch a glimpse of pornography in any format. But the fact is I did. And it made an impact on me.

The sexual overtones that colored my life from the time I was only a few years old sometimes manifested in the way I played with other kids. This was true when I was five and it was true when I got older. I got caught playing naked under the porch with one of the neighborhood boys and once underneath the bed with a boy from school. For some reason, I was always getting caught naked with a boy.

When I reached my early teens, a group of neighborhood boys and I would head over to an abandoned warehouse down the block to play strip poker or any other card games that required taking off our clothes. I was the only girl. So the prize? Me. Whoever won got to pretend to have sex with me naked.

There was obviously a connection between my abandonment issues and the sexual abuse. On one hand, I craved physical affection—not in a perverse way but as a form of pure, unconditional love. On the other hand, I still guarded my heart and was adept at unplugging when things got distressing. In the moments of abuse, I learned how to clench my eyes tight and hold my breath until it was over. I tried not to think about how uncomfortable and scared I was or how I wanted to crawl inside of myself and disappear. I just held on for dear life to emptiness, a blank mind and a heart void of feelings. Though my experiences taught me to shut down and push aside the things I really wanted, I couldn't escape the unrequited desire to be unconditionally loved the way I wanted—for the love I needed from my dad.

Three

Though it had been years since I'd seen him, I missed my dad. I wanted him back. Since I was a little girl, I had waited for the day the phone would ring and it would be him. I had the script memorized. He'd be flooded with remorse and regret for leaving us, and he'd tell me how much he loved me and that he was coming back and staying for good. He'd repeat "I'm sorry" until the words mended my broken heart and rid me of the sadness I had carried all those years.

By the time I was nine, I had just a pinch of hope left. I still loosely held on to the fantasy of being rescued by him, especially because I had not connected on an emotional level with any other adult, including my mom or stepdad.

I came home from school one day that year and bounced through the front door. On my way to the kitchen to grab a snack, I noticed my mom sitting on the couch with a strange man. They spoke quietly. The tension was obvious. My mom's shoulders were uncomfortably stiff and the man looked nervous.

When she saw me, my mom stood up and smoothed her pants. "Pattie," she began in a monotone voice. "This is Mike . . . your father." The tall, skinny man beside my mother stood up. He seemed to tower over me like a giant. He looked nervous and kept fiddling with his hands. This was him? The man I'd waited for my whole life?

I blinked. A lot. I was caught off guard. No matter how many times I had pictured this moment in my head, I wasn't prepared. I wasn't sure how to react. I definitely felt a jolt of excitement; the butterflies in my stomach were flying into each other. But I couldn't move. My feet were glued to the floor.

My dad looked into my eyes and smiled. "Hello, Pattie," he said with kindness. I don't remember us having a moment anything like the daydream I had reserved in my head for the past seven years. Although we didn't have a palpable connection, there was no extreme awkwardness between us. Our company was comfortable enough to warrant a pleasant dinner that evening with my brother, Chris. The three of us even went to the mall afterward, and my dad bought me a soft E.T. doll. I was thrilled. It replaced Thumbelina, who had been hijacked and destroyed by my brother not long after my dad gave her to me.

That night my dad returned home to Timmins, a ten-hour drive away, but he promised to keep in touch. After the shock wore off, I was beside myself. My dad was back. I was on cloud nine that I was going to have a relationship with him. I mattered again. This was my moment, and nothing could take him away from me. Nothing.

My dad kept his promise. I remember getting phone calls from him every now and then. He even mailed me the best gift ever. I had been begging my mom for cable TV in my room, but we didn't have a cable outfit upstairs. My father mailed me the longest cable cord I have ever seen in my entire life so I could connect my TV to the downstairs line. My mother wasn't happy because the cable had to run from the first floor living room up the stairs, through the hall, and into my room. I, on the other hand, was ecstatic. Cable in my room! Wow!

A few months after my dad's visit, my brother had made plans to spend the summer with my dad, his wife, and his extended family. On the morning Chris was supposed to leave, my mom got a phone call. It was only six thirty in the morning. I didn't hear the phone ring, but I did hear the door to my bedroom creak open and my mom walk over to my bed. I was groggy, still in a sleep fog.

"Pattie, I'm sorry," she told me. "Your father died last night. He had a heart attack." She told me my brother had already left for Timmins and would attend the funeral.

It was peculiar. I felt nothing. It was like almost at the sound of those words, the finality of the statement, my heart instantly turned off. Every bit of hope that had stemmed from being reunited with my dad vanished. As I'd done time and time again in the past, I detached myself emotionally to protect myself from feeling anything at all. I became completely disconnected to keep myself safe from even the slightest bit of emotion. I did, however, feel sorry for my mom and ask her if she was okay. She, of course, was fine. I allowed myself to be led by her example, so I too was fine. No muss. No fuss.

Six years later, some of the volcanic emotions that had been buried that day started steaming their way to the surface. I went to visit my dad's tombstone in Timmins. Most of our relatives on both sides lived there, so our family made the drive at least once a year to visit. On a clear sunny day, absent of any noise outside of a landscaper trimming nearby bushes, I stood in front of his grave and yelled at the top of my lungs.

For about an hour, I screamed at the inanimate slab of stone in hopes of surfacing the emotions I knew were inside of me. I was angry but not full of rage, though I knew the rage existed some-where. I had spent my life stuffing down emotion, shoving aside my hurts and pains, pushing legitimate feelings down so deep that apparently even I couldn't dig them out, not even by staring at the tombstone bearing my father's name. I yelled at him for leaving me too early, for abandoning me twice, but even as the words flew out of my mouth in a verbal storm, I didn't emotionally connect. I was still so far removed from the deep part of my heart.

My internal walls had been firmly reinforced by abuse and disappointment. The emotional disconnect was my obvious defense strategy, the only way I could continue living a normal (whatever that means) life. Abuse? Disconnect. Emotionally absent mom? Disconnect. Dad dies? Disconnect. It wasn't long before those defenses worked against me. Being a pro at disconnecting did, however, give me one advantage.

My ability to disconnect from reality helped fuel my love for the arts, especially acting. I always thought I was going to be an actress. When I was around nine, I made appearances on *Romper Room* and *Big Top Talent*, a Canadian television children's talent show where I recited a monologue from *Anne of Green Gables* and told the story of Jack and the Beanstalk. I was a ham who loved not just the camera but pretending I was someone else.

I'm sure I gravitated toward playing characters because it allowed me to step away from what was happening to me. Acting also gave me a sense of control. I could use my voice to make people laugh or cry. I could be as loud and dramatic as I wanted. I also loved to sing. All through middle school and high school, I took every drama and choir class that was offered. I was in the school choir every year and had major roles in almost every school play. I was quite literally a drama queen. I also spent seven years taking dance lessons. I couldn't get enough of the arts.

When I was ten, I performed in the Stratford Shakespeare Festival, a celebration of the theatrical arts that runs from April to November every year. More than half a million tourists from all over the world visit our little town during that time to see wonderful performances of plays by Shakespeare and other greats. I was cast for two roles in *The Government Inspector* and played a peasant girl and a rich girl.

I loved the hustle backstage before the performance—sitting in the hair and makeup chair, wearing frilly costumes, being doted on by the older actresses. But being onstage thrilled me even more. It gave me a sense of freedom. My heart wasn't burdened by feelings of abandonment, fear, or rejection or by those wretched dirty feelings I still didn't understand. I was free to act, to be dramatic and perform from a place in my spirit that captured innocence. I was unfettered as a kite.

Throughout elementary and junior high school, I filled up my bedroom with awards and trophies from singing and acting competitions. I even got accepted into an acting agency in Toronto, but it required me going to auditions on the weekend. My mom and Bruce refused to make the hour-and-a-half drive, so I couldn't go. I was devastated. It was the one chance I'd had to hone something I was actually really good at. My dreams were crushed.

As much as I loved acting and drawing from different identities and personas when I was younger, I still couldn't escape how others were violating my body. You can't fake an accent to cover shame. It was hard to reconcile the sexual abuse that had been happening to me since I was a little girl. Even though I've since been through intensive counseling and healing, even today certain memories and feelings don't just go away. There are still moments when I can see the little girl in me crouching low in the shadows, afraid, unheard, confused, ashamed.

When I sought counseling many years after the abuse, I learned from my therapist that young victims of trauma carry those wounds, most of them covered up and even deeply buried, into adulthood. As a little girl, I did what I had to do to adapt in my abusive environment. Because I did so, however, the five-year-old me never had the opportunity to address the injustices. I couldn't voice how abandoned I felt. Or how hurt. Or how betrayed. Or how ashamed. I never had the chance.

During one of my visits, my counselor recommended an exercise where I, as an adult, could visualize my younger self during this traumatic time and walk through some of the pain. The older me could defend and even protect the younger me who felt alone. She told me I needed to mentally travel back to the age when the abuse first showed up. The adult had to connect with the child, no matter how painful it was. I had to go back in time and allow the little girl to talk. I had to give her a voice.

My initial reaction was to say no. Revisit my inner child? Please. It sounded like psychobabble. However, my reluctance almost always gave way to trying different exercises, even if they lay outside my comfort zone.

So one day in my therapist's office, I closed my eyes and pictured myself as a five-year-old girl. I was surprised at how rapidly the vision in my mind unfolded. A little girl sat on a bed and hugged her knobby knees to her chest, rocking back and forth as if in slow motion. Long, straight, dark hair with a heavy bang framed her delicate features. Normally bright and clear, her greenish-blue eyes looked dull and lifeless, aimed at the floor. I noticed her shoulders sagged, weighed down by a burden too heavy to bear.

I asked the younger Pattie if I could sit with her for a bit, and she said yes. We sat in silence for a few minutes, and then I heard a soft whimpering. Faint drops of tears cascaded down her tiny cheeks. I asked her what was wrong. "My mommy doesn't love me," she whispered.

For the record, I don't remember feeling unloved as a little girl. My mother wasn't a bad or abusive mom who neglected me. On the contrary, I know she worked hard and did the best she could at raising me. I don't think that was necessarily the point of my reconnection with my five-year-old self. I feel I simply had to acknowledge the hurting and confused child in me. I had to comfort her, to tell her that everything would be okay. And most of all, I had to allow her to exercise her voice—the voice I never knew I had. The voice I finally found when someone told me it was okay to say no.

I was ten when a thirty-second public service announcement (PSA) helped me gain enough power to turn the tables on all the abuse I had been experiencing up to that point. I was mindlessly watching TV when a pint-sized African American boy whom I recognized as

Webster from the TV show of the same name talked to me as he moved through a set of giant, colorful letters of the alphabet.

My ears started ringing when I heard, "Sometimes grownups touch kids in ways they don't like."

It was the first time I had ever heard someone verbalize exactly what I had been feeling for the last five-plus years. This kid knew how I felt. My heart started beating wildly in my chest. I thought it was going to break through my skin and take off like a rocket. Then I heard the voice of another little kid in the background who mentioned something about his uncle touching him in an icky way. *Yes!* I wanted to shout through the screen. *Yes, that's right! It feels icky. It feels gross.*

The kid continued to talk about feeling funny when someone touches you and tells you not to tell anyone else. And then Emmanuel Lewis said the magic words that gave me a semblance of control. That gave me a way to put a stop to the abuse. That gave me my voice.

"Say no. Then go. And tell someone you trust."

My mind raced. So many different thoughts cluttered my brain in that moment. *All I have to do is say no? Is it really that easy? Will it work?*

I was nervous but desperate enough to try it out. I knew the touching had to stop. My stomach churned when I thought about it. I had to wait for an opportunity to say no. I had to wait to be touched in that awful way.

I sat numbly in front of the TV as the show I was watching earlier continued in an indistinct blur of colors and sounds. Fears began to manipulate my mind. I started to think of all the reasons I shouldn't say no and should continue my MO and keep quiet, not rocking the boat. *What if I say no and he gets mad? What if me saying no makes him get violent? What if I say no and he rejects me and never talks to me again?* But my biggest fear was, *What if it just doesn't work?*

In the end, my desperation to put an end to the abuse overrode my anxiety. I knew I had to do it. I knew I had to say no. The PSA gave me just enough courage to try.

One day it happened. My original molester cornered me and initiated the familiar routine of peeling off my clothes and taking turns touching. Before he could do anything further, though, I mustered up all the courage I could find and meekly said, "No. I don't want this to happen anymore." My voice was barely above a whisper, as loud as I was able to speak, but make no mistake, it was clear.

Then I said it again, this time a tiny notch louder.

"No."

What happened next amazes me to this day. He nodded, said "Okay," and walked out of the room. He never touched me again.

I found myself in the same situation again a few weeks later, with the other longtime offender. When that young man started his own ritual with me, I whispered my conviction in that same subdued voice. "No," I told him, just as I had the other guy. "I don't want to do this anymore." And with that, he never again laid a hand on me.

Finally, I had found my voice. And I found bits and pieces of just enough strength to use it.

What I didn't do, however, was tell anyone about it. I didn't understand why I had to tell someone I trusted. None of my abusers had ever explicitly told me not to tell anyone. I just didn't. Why would I want to, anyway? There was no need for someone else to know about my unbearable shame.

During the few seconds it took to say no, I was a part of the present. I wasn't distant. I didn't unplug. I didn't close my eyes and pretend time had stopped and bad things weren't happening. I acknowledged that things weren't right. That what was happening to me had to stop.

While the word *no* was my permission slip to speak up and defend myself, I quickly learned the word wasn't magic. It worked to stop the abuse from occurring, but it didn't release me from my emotional turmoil. Emotions that I kept at bay. Emotions that multiplied and mutated as time passed.

When I'd feel sad, my instinct to cry was overpowering, but an even stronger part told me to zip it. When I'd feel afraid, I'd want to reach out for help, but I'd remind myself it was better to ignore it. It took a long while for me to reconcile my voice and my heart.

Four

I spent most of my early teen years in my bedroom, zoned out from the rest of the world and from my dark memories. I buried my head in my journals, where I would furiously write about how life sucked and how miserable I was. It was the genesis of my depression, bouts of which lasted well into my adulthood. I didn't know how to deal with my pain, so I wrote poem after poem, every one of them telling the story of a girl with a broken heart. My words painted the picture of a teenage identity crisis, my obvious depression, and hints of confusion about my sexual trauma.

> I try so hard
> To be what others want me to be.
> I am forever being someone else,
> And for this, I know not who I am . . .
> It hurts to pretend.
> I feel as if I don't fit in anywhere . . .

I am responsible for things I do and decisions I make,
But wrong choices are made and disaster occurs.
When things are built up inside,
Whether it be frustration, anger, or confusion,
The thought of suicide is possible to occur . . .

No one knew the kinds of destructive things that festered in my heart. Outside of seeing me act out in rebellion, in small spurts at first, my family probably didn't even have a clue something was wrong. You want the ones who are supposed to love you the most, even unconditionally, to take the time to look beyond your messy parts or rough edges, but I didn't feel like my mom or stepdad were interested in doing that. I guess it's hard enough to parent a teenager, let alone decipher the hieroglyphics of a broken one.

Aside from sitting at the table during meals, our family rarely spent time together. By this time all my siblings were out of the house, so at times I felt pretty lonely at home. I may not have acted like it at the time, but I wanted to do stuff as a family, even if it was just Bruce, my mom, and me. We could take bike rides. Or have game night. Or go to a sporting event. But we didn't do much other than watching TV.

Communication wasn't a big deal in our family. Outside of small talk about mundane topics like the weather or school, we really didn't talk a whole lot. We definitely didn't express many emotions openly with each other.

One afternoon after school, I sat at the kitchen table mindlessly munching on ketchup chips (popular in Canada) when the phone rang.

"Hello?"

"Chris Zehr got into a car accident," said a friend of mine on the phone, panting breathlessly. "He's dead."

I gulped. A wave of disbelief rushed over me. Memories started flooding my mind. I had known Chris since I was three or four. We had the same babysitter and were super close early on in elementary school. He was at my birthday party every year when we were kids.

We'd drifted apart over the years but kept in touch every now and then. I thought about his mom. She was a single mom and Chris was her only child. How could fate be so cruel?

I threw the phone down on its cradle and ran upstairs to my room. The news knocked the wind out of me. I couldn't breathe. I threw myself on the bed and physically felt grief inching its way through every crack in my heart. My sadness paved a way to other emotions, deeper ones I didn't understand. I sobbed hysterically and made such a ruckus that Bruce heard the commotion. He knocked on my bedroom door and opened it, looking more annoyed than concerned.

"What's the problem, Pattie?"

"I'm sad," I managed to blurt out between the heaving sobs that shook my shoulders. "My friend just died."

Bruce let out an exasperated sigh. "Oh, stop that. My friend Jimmy died a few weeks ago. You didn't see me crying and acting a mess, now did you?"

I blinked through my tears, stunned speechless. Weren't you supposed to cry when someone died? (In hindsight, perhaps Bruce, like my mom, was uncomfortable with deep emotions and didn't know how else to respond. I know he didn't like to see me upset.)

I talked to my mom later that day and told her what happened. I wanted her permission to feel sad. I needed her to tell me it was okay to cry. "Mom, Bruce said I shouldn't be upset."

My mom looked uneasy. It was a conversation that may have required kid gloves, but the emotional undertones were quickly cut off. "Well, when Sally died, that's what people told me. They said crying was just a way to feel sorry for yourself."

Looking back on it now, what she said is heartbreaking. How sad that my mother was probably never able to properly grieve the loss of her daughter in an emotional way. How could she have encouraged me that it was okay to cry if it wasn't okay for her to?

Mom wasn't a naturally touchy-feely person and didn't show much emotion. She was direct and matter-of-fact. Unfortunately, as a result, what could have been a teachable moment or an opportunity for her to console me was shut down. It was another reminder to hush up. Feelings were useless, and anything that could give rise to feelings should be ignored, buried, or superficially glossed over. Period.

I know my mother recognized the tension between us. She even admitted at times her inability to relate to or talk to me. But recognizing the tension didn't fix it.

Like any child who has been through a traumatic experience, I was left screaming on the inside from the repeated bouts of molestation I'd experienced. I wanted so badly to reach out and purge everything that had been locked inside my spirit, all the ugliness and all the shame. I was dying to tell my mother about the injustices I had faced, about feeling alone, about being scared. But I didn't know how to.

Unfortunately, I didn't know how to articulate those deep feelings, so most of what I *did* say came out as yelling and was disrespectful. Sometimes I approached my mom with tears in my eyes after I got into a fight with one of my friends or was bullied, but her response was always the same. Time and time again she told me, "I don't know how to do this, Pattie. My mom never talked to me, so I don't know how to talk to you. Just talk to a guidance counselor or one of your friends' moms. I love you, but I just can't talk to you."

And that was that.

Although my mom lacked in communication or affection, she excelled at performance. I can see now that her "love language" is "acts of service" (*The Five Love Languages* by Gary Chapman is one of my favorite books; read it to find out yours). That means she shows love by doing things for others.

While I was growing up, Mom worked full-time in a factory. But she always came home and made time to cook for us, do laundry, get what we needed for school, make sure the house was in order, and provide what she could that we needed. (My mom still loves to do these things for me when I visit with her in Canada.)

Today I can appreciate the backdrop behind my mom's way of being, but as a teenager, the fact is, it hurt. I couldn't approach her about things that were important to me. Like how I felt when my dad left; that was a big one. His leaving was traumatic. I didn't understand what was happening, and I didn't get an explanation. He was here one minute and gone the next.

Because my mom didn't acknowledge my feelings of confusion, I didn't feel she was a safe place to use my voice. Whenever I would talk to her about something that was bothering me, I'd have the gnawing feeling I was more of a burden to her than simply a child who needed her mom. So I quickly decided it was better to leave her alone.

Along the way I came to some pretty unhealthy conclusions: I wasn't important. My feelings weren't valid. My thoughts didn't matter. So I learned how to cope with what I couldn't handle on my own by stuffing it inside. I locked the most upsetting and traumatizing events in a place so deep, I hoped I'd never be able to dig them out.

When I was in the eighth grade, I started hanging out with the wrong group of girls—the ones who were always getting in trouble for something. Stealing was our cheap thrill. We especially got a kick out of stealing ketchup chips and Zesty Cheese Doritos out of the school cafeteria. I know, big deal! (Wanna hear a really embarrassing secret between you and me? My friends and I called ourselves the Chipettes. How cheesy is that?)

The six of us were big shots, rebels without a clue. We were joined at the hip and did everything together. We had slumber parties. We swapped clothes. We pined after cute boys. We complained about our parents. We shared our disdain for school. And, of course, we got off on our small-town criminal activity, like stealing chips and, when we were feeling super cocky, cheap red lipsticks from the local drugstore. Five of us also loved to sing and were involved with the school tour choir.

One day the choir was scheduled to perform a concert at a huge mall in London, Ontario. People all over the mall—making their way through the food court, hustling in and out of department stores to rummage through clearance racks, and dragging reluctant husbands and whiny children up and down the escalators—would hear our melodic repertoire, like my all-time favorite, Chicago's "You're the Inspiration." The five of us were excited about performing, but mostly we were psyched about spending a school day at a mall.

I sensed something weird on the bus ride there. I sat on a two-seater by myself while my best friends sat across from me. The girls chatted away in their private world, leaning into each other at such an angle that I couldn't help but feel they were ignoring me. They nodded my way every so often as I tried to force my way into their conversation. They were polite but curt. It felt awkward. And I felt left out.

Did I do something wrong? Did I say something wrong?

As the bus bounced along the highway, the massive billboards and gray office buildings flashing by, my hurt feelings festered. I ignored the rest of the choir as they loudly belted out their singing parts, preparing for the big debut. When the bus finally rolled into the mall parking lot, my friends barged their way to the front of the bus, leaving me to quicken my pace to keep up.

We had an hour to walk around before we had to meet to line up for the concert. The teachers barked out orders, reminding us not to be even a minute late, then finally gave us permission to go. We were like stallions being released into the wild, or in this case, into an endless array of stores where we could salivate over a pair of Doc Martens, blinding-patterned Hammer pants, or the latest Guns N' Roses CD.

While I stood in the middle of my best friends, I couldn't ignore the tension, like they were almost forcing themselves to be in my presence. I noticed they were looking at each other with knowing glances. Finally they nudged one of the girls forward to face me. She looked sheepish, uncomfortable, and couldn't look into my eyes. It was obvious she didn't want to say what she was about to but knew there was no way around it.

"We don't want to hang out with you today, Pattie." She paused and raised her eyes to the ceiling before letting out a deep sigh. "And, well, we don't want you to hang out with us anymore or be our friend."

The words punched me in the gut. The blow was so sharp, it punctured a hole in the protective layer I had built over the years to defend against rejection and abandonment. The wound traveled further and deeper than just being told someone didn't want to be my friend. It struck a familiar chord at a level I didn't even know existed. My eyes welled with tears.

Another one of my so-called friends quickly piped up. She sounded more confident and not at all apologetic. "Yeah, and don't go crying like a baby."

I panicked. My mind went into overdrive. "What did I do wrong?" I asked. "Was it something I said? Or did? Give me a chance to fix it. I'm so sorry . . ." My voice trailed off in a stuttering mess of apologies. I felt like they had just poured a pound of salt over the already open wound of rejection.

Just as the tears were about to descend, I clenched my jaw and used every ounce of strength I could muster to keep myself from crying. I was proud of myself. My eyes welled so much I could barely see, but not one tear dropped. Not one.

I knew what I had to do: Pull myself up. Be strong. Keep it together. Pretend as if that conversation never happened. It was the story of my life—building up ever greater walls to shut down my emotions. I ended up walking around by myself, aimlessly wandering through the mall. I was devastated. Utterly and absolutely devastated.

Though it may seem like a silly event, it wielded enough power to stick with me through the years. It confirmed, in my mind, that I wasn't important. That I didn't matter. That nobody wanted me, not even my best friends.

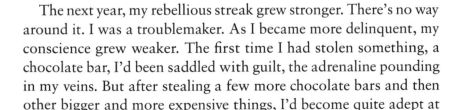

The next year, my rebellious streak grew stronger. There's no way around it. I was a troublemaker. As I became more delinquent, my conscience grew weaker. The first time I had stolen something, a chocolate bar, I'd been saddled with guilt, the adrenaline pounding in my veins. But after stealing a few more chocolate bars and then other bigger and more expensive things, I'd become quite adept at ignoring the guilt, so much so that it eventually faded to an inaudible lull. I kept telling myself that what I was doing wasn't wrong, and I slowly began to desensitize my conscience.

Though I kept pushing boundaries with authority figures, picking fights with teachers and spending most of my after school hours in detention, I moved on to bigger and badder things. I started vandalizing school property; one time I even got suspended for starting a fire in a bathroom.

Then came the drugs and alcohol.

I started drinking alcohol and smoking pot when I was fourteen. There were more parties than I knew what to do with, and every one of them featured some type of mind-numbing substance. I can't remember the first time I drank or smoked pot. It must not have been that interesting of an experience. Since all of my friends were drinking and drugging, it was easy to get sucked in with the crowd, and no one needed to twist my arm to try anything at least once. Besides, Stratford was such a small city. It's easy to get bored when there's not much to do. Drugs and alcohol were like an extracurricular activity. It seemed harmless at first—just feeling loopy and doing stupid things. Getting high made life more interesting.

Around the same time I started experimenting with drugs and alcohol, an old ghost came back into town. It had been about four years since anyone had touched me inappropriately. Four years that I had successfully kept most of the remnants of the abuse swept under the proverbial rug. But now the phantom was back for more.

I was fourteen years old, it was summer, and I was hanging out with my best friend, one of the infamous Chipettes. We had become fast friends in kindergarten and lived across the street from one another. We were inseparable. When we got old enough to have phones in our rooms, we'd call each other right when we woke up, even before meeting in front of my house to walk together to school.

"How are you?"

"What are you doing?"

"What's new?"

And as our heads hit the pillow at night, we'd dial each other and end the evening with more meaningless BFF conversation.

"How are you?"

"What are you doing?"

"Anything new?"

We were like sisters, and I often spent time with her family. That summer we spent a week in the great outdoors on a camping adventure with her grandfather and sister. I had seen him around a lot and always felt comfortable with him. He was the kind of grandfather everyone loved—super cuddly and soft, like a big teddy bear you just wanted to wrap your arms around.

Because I didn't get as much affection as I needed at home (my love languages are physical touch and words of affirmation), I craved physical attention. It was how I felt loved. Adored. Accepted.

So I loved hanging out with my friend's grandfather. He was warm and caring, and he loved to give hugs. Because I was so tiny—only four foot six and maybe seventy pounds at the time—there were even times I'd curl up in his lap. It was easy for me to sit on this man's lap without it feeling physically awkward.

My friend and I spent the first few days of our vacation enjoying nature. We rode bikes, took long hikes, and swam in the campground pool. At night we sat around an inviting fire roasting marshmallows and listening to music.

One afternoon I saw my friend's grandfather sitting on a huge lawn chair, staring into the sky and enjoying the warm breeze. He looked so peaceful. Content. Just breathing in the summer without a care in the world. I wanted to be a part of that beautiful picture, part of the equation of peaceful nothingness.

I climbed onto his lap and rested my head in the crook of his leathery neck. He smiled, eyes still closed, and patted my head reassuringly. It wasn't long before I started drifting off to sleep.

And then I felt it—the heat from his warm hand. The movement startled me, and my reverie came to a grinding halt.

It was happening again.

I was unable to fully process it all as his hand slowly and deliberately groped its way inside my shorts, resting where it didn't belong and touching me in a way he shouldn't have. *Oh no. Not this. Please, God.* As deep as my feeling of disgust was, I was also scared. Scared of rejecting him. Scared of saying no and risking him hating me. I thought, *How am I going to get out of this situation without offending this sweet old man?* Do you see how warped the thought process of a sexual abuse victim can be? It's a battle I could never win.

I let out a fake yawn and inconspicuously stretched, as if I had just woken up from a catnap. I shifted my body away from his lap so I ended up sitting more on the chair than on his legs. Then I yawned again, got up, and stumbled away, pretending I was still drowsy. I hoped my act was enough to diffuse the unsettling situation.

I walked back to the camper, the sun blinding me and blasting me with its heat. I felt as if I were trudging through a barren desert, miles away from civilization. The truth was, I was miles away from myself. Once again, I detached from the colorful scene in front of me. I could barely make out the families grilling food, the little kids tossing Frisbees, the worn hikers returning from their long walk. I walked in a fog, stunned by what had just happened.

The old familiar feelings came back as if they had never left. Rather, they'd been hiding under the surface, waiting for the perfect time to reappear. Patterns in my brain immediately reconnected with my past abuse, transporting me back in time, and the floodgates of all the old memories unleashed with fury. The event was so upsetting, I tried to convince myself the incident was a fluke. Maybe I had imagined it all.

But I didn't dream it up. It happened. And I finally found enough courage in that moment to tell someone.

When I got back to the camper, I pulled aside my friend and told her and her sister what had happened. My friend chewed her gum loudly, looking at me with a half-cocked eyebrow. I had the feeling she was suspicious. No, it was worse. As soon as I noticed the first sign of her head shaking, I knew she didn't believe me.

Popping a huge bubble right in front of my face, the sticky gum only inches away from exploding on my suntanned cheek, she looked at me with contempt and accused me of lying. Her sister was just as vocal about me being a liar.

I didn't expect that kind of a response. Their reaction devastated me. The PSA I'd seen all those years ago hadn't prepared me for the possibility that I could tell someone but they wouldn't believe me. What then? How do you handle being called a liar when you are the victim?

My mistrust of others grew in that moment. The conversation also taught me a valuable lesson. Though I was pretty confident I would never again talk about stuff like that, I knew that if I did, I'd choose my confidante wisely. It wouldn't be someone close to the offender. I would need someone who wouldn't automatically come to their defense.

I wanted to leave the campground immediately after opening up to my friend, but for some reason I stayed. I tried my best to brush off the incident and was determined to pull myself together and act as if everything was fine. I was used to spending time around my abusers, pretending nothing had ever happened, so it was easy to do. *What dirty old man?*

The four of us played cards later that night. As I was waiting for my turn in our second round of Crazy Eights, I felt a hand slither up my leg and stop below the end of my zipper. It was the grandpa. *Okay. That's it. Enough is enough.* Still not wanting to make a scene, I got up and said I wasn't feeling well and was going to bed. I didn't want—or rather I didn't know how—to handle the situation any other way. I would just take myself out of the picture, and no one would be the wiser. What was I going to say, anyway? "Your grandfather's trying to cop a feel again. See? I told you I wasn't lying." No one would have believed me, and there was no way I was getting involved in a he-said, she-said argument.

So I did what was most comfortable—I retreated.

I think that happens a lot with abuse victims. Instead of using our voice to speak out, we keep quiet. We hide. We ignore. We pretend. There are so many different reasons we don't tell others. We don't want to rock the boat. We don't want to make anyone mad. What if they think we asked for it? What if we look stupid? What if they think we're lying? It's such a difficult and delicate thing with which to wrestle.

Though it feels like talking carries too much of a risk, in the process of keeping silent, we dig a deeper grave for ourselves day by day. By shouldering the burden alone, we are forced to find other outlets, usually unhealthy ones, to help us deal with it. Most times they lead us further down a dark road, making it harder to find our way up.

As a teen, I envied people who could be unguarded, unafraid. I even wrote about that in my journal: "I think [I'm getting] more open with my feelings. I wish someone could understand what I'm going through. In drama class, everyone is so open. Girls told the class how they got abused sexually and a couple raped. It was so sad. Everyone was crying."

Yet in the next sentence, I made a sharp U-turn from writing about being vulnerable and wrote, "I hate how people are popular because they are pretty." It was a stark about-face. There was no transition. I was so removed from the pain in my past, not even my diary was privy to the deep waters.

———

Not long after the camping incident, I was drinking and doing drugs every day. I was getting into even more trouble at school and going to parties almost every night. I rarely ate dinner at home, and I never made curfew. Some nights I even stayed out until the early hours of the morning.

Getting drunk and high for fun turned into a means of self-medicating. I couldn't get through a class at school or a holiday function with my family without being stoned or drunk. By the time I was sixteen, I couldn't function at all without numbing myself in some way.

I stuck mostly with pot, my tried-and-true friend, though at times I had a feeling the joints I smoked were laced with angel dust or cocaine. I also did LSD. My trips were racked with paranoia and fear. I would feel unrelenting anxiety during the twelve-hour high.

If I took a hit before school, I was a goner the entire day. I'd sit in class and try to follow what the teacher was saying, but I'd forget everything two seconds after she said it. Same thing with reading. I'd run my finger along a sentence, and by the time I got to the end of the line, I had no clue what I'd just read. If I was walking down the hall at school and saw the principal, I was convinced he was walking past me straight to my locker. He'd open the metal closet, find my stash of drugs, and have me arrested. The police would then drag me kicking and screaming out of the school and throw me in prison, where I'd spend the rest of my life. A little extreme? Sure. Welcome to the world of LSD.

My mom wasn't stupid. She noticed my strange behavior. Though she would get upset if I came home drunk or high, she didn't press the issue. She would occasionally question me about using drugs or alcohol, and I'd always lie and say I wasn't doing that stuff. She'd let it go.

Though my mom and I didn't see each other much because I was either out partying or holed up in my room, when we did, World War III tended to break out. All the pent-up emotions that had been building in me since I was a little girl spewed mini volcanoes during these arguments. My rage came out in bits and pieces, and unfortunately my mom took the brunt of my temper. Once it even got physical.

I can't remember what we were arguing about. It kept escalating at a pace neither one of us could stop. Heated words were exchanged like a ball in a Ping-Pong match. At one point I got in my mom's face, my small features contorting with rage. It was too close for comfort. She took a step back and slapped me. The blow made me even more livid, and I threatened to call the cops. I even grabbed the telephone and with a menacing look on my face yelled, "That's it, I'm dialing!"

My mother wasn't one to back down. She called my bluff and grabbed me by the wrist, pulling me toward the front door. "I have a better idea. I'll take you down to the police station myself." And she did.

Down at the station, I had a sit-down with one of the police officers. He talked to me about the importance of respecting my parents, respecting myself, and getting good grades. He was nice, though I can't say his talk made me change my ways or even scared me, as my mother had probably intended.

That was my first experience with the police, but it wouldn't be my last. It wasn't too long before the police started showing up at my house when things like car stereos went missing. They knew the kind of friends I hung out with and the kind of stuff we did.

My mother and I had such a volatile relationship that we tried counseling a few times. I loved those meetings. I was able to talk to my mom about how I really felt with the support of a therapist. I also felt defended when the counselor would call my mom out on a few things. Of course, she also did the same with me. It was clear that my mom and I both had our issues, which made it difficult for us to relate. And while counseling didn't lessen the tension between us, at the very least it gave me an outlet.

I used to love visiting our neighbors next door because being in their company brought me a sense of comfort I needed at the time. It was a respite from the drama at home. They were Christian people, or as my mom liked to call them, "religious folk."

Though Mom would roll her eyes at their Jesus talk, I didn't mind hearing them talk about God. I was intrigued by the Bible verses that hung on their walls. I asked questions. I wanted to know what the verses meant, what the Bible was about. This couple embraced my curiosity and never hesitated to spend time sharing with me what they knew. They also often prayed for my family and me, prayers I have no doubt made an impact on where I am today.

But despite the testimonies of this couple, I had no real personal connection to God. He wasn't on my radar outside of the kind of desperate prayers we pray when we're at the end of our rope. Like the times when I was drunk to the point of being violently sick. As I'd puke my guts out into the toilet, I'd cling to my porcelain friend for dear life. "God," I'd cry out as my insides felt they were being mashed through a meat grinder. "If You make me feel better, I promise I'll never drink or do drugs again." I can't tell you how many times I found myself in front of a toilet bowl, sick as a dog, convinced I had alcohol poisoning. And I repeated these prayers more times than I can count.

Of course, I felt better eventually. But I never stopped drinking or using drugs. Were those prayers simply a desperate measure for a desperate time? Mostly, they probably were. But I also think I held on to an iota of hope that God was real. That He existed. That far beyond the four walls of the bathroom where I was disgustingly sick, there was Someone out there. Someone who even actually cared.

I do believe that the bits and pieces of faith I picked up along the way, however small, made lasting impressions on my heart. Though invisible to the naked eye, God left behind His fingerprints, evidence that He was there. That He was real. But I didn't know that then. I only knew pain and emptiness.

I hadn't a clue what God was like. Without a spiritual foundation, I imagined Him to be someone He is not. I forged an image based on lies. I didn't know any better. When God is referred to as a heavenly Father, our earthly perceptions of what a parent is like (based on our experiences with our own parents) often taint our view of God.

Because my parents were distant, I imagined God was too. Because my father left, I imagined God as one who could, at any moment, decide to walk away. Because no one rescued me from my abuse, I imagined God as sitting on the sidelines, unable or unwilling to rescue me from injustice. It certainly didn't seem as though He cared.

Five

When your true self—who God created you to be—is broken into unrecognizable fragments, you become fertile soil for lies. As those untruths get buried deeper and deeper into your heart, it's almost impossible to get rid of them. They are so securely lodged there that they become a part of you that you cannot imagine living without.

I was bound by so many lies by the time I was a teenager. At best, I had a skewed idea of love, worth, and self-respect; at worst, I had none. Instead of believing in myself, I knelt at the merciless feet of deceit, hanging on to every negative word spoken to me and entertaining every taunting thought of my own that surfaced in my mind.

I recently read journal entries from my teen years, and I can't believe the things I called myself. *Lazy. Fat. Ugly.* I even concluded someone must have been brain damaged to like me. When a boyfriend called me a loser or a slut, I had no truth with which to defend myself against the verbal assaults, whether they came from others or me, so they stuck like a mosquito in honey. I was so used to being taken advantage of as a little girl, I didn't know how else to be treated. I wouldn't have known true love if it socked me between the eyes.

When it came to guys, I was always trying to find "the one." But I couldn't seem to make up my mind. I liked Guy X one week, Guy Y the next, and so on. I especially gravitated toward the boys who liked me first; they were the ones who would pretty much guarantee me some kind of affection.

I didn't flip-flop from one guy to the next simply because my teenage hormones were out of control, though. I was always searching, trying to find love. Trying to find something real. Trying to find the person who would love me back the way I thought I needed. Getting that from a guy seemed the easiest solution.

I fell in love—or like, or whatever it was—easily. And when it didn't last, I was crushed, nursing those wounds for a long time. When I was fifteen, I found a boy I thought I was going to marry. I'll call him Joey.

I liked this kid a lot. One night after everyone left a party at his house, we sat and cuddled for hours. In the still of the early morning, he started saying all the things a girl wants to hear. "Pattie, you are so beautiful." "You're so soft." "You're so amazing." I swallowed his sweet nothings hook, line, and sinker. I was a hopeless romantic, and his words made me weak in the knees.

We started kissing and ended up in his bedroom. I was nervous. I didn't want this to end the way it was obviously going. Despite the amount of abuse I had endured, I was still a virgin. That part of me was precious and innocent. I wasn't ready to give it up yet, not even to Joey.

As we fooled around on the bed, he started trying to take off my clothes, slowly and inconspicuously. My body tightened. I squirmed around to get his hands away from certain areas on my body, but it was no use; he was much stronger than I was.

"No, Joey," I said, still fidgeting in the mesh of our intertwining legs and arms. "I don't want to do this."

He whispered in my ear, "Don't worry. I'm not going to hurt you."

I kept repeating "No," and Joey kept saying, "It's okay." I didn't yell. I didn't scream. I didn't beat him off me. But I said no. I said it so many times I numbly reverted back into abuse mode. I was still. Silent. Detached from my body. Detached from Joey. Detached from time. I just wanted to get the inevitable over with.

When it was over, I reconnected my body with my mind. I plugged my emotions back in. Though I didn't know it at the time, delusion set in. I repainted the scenario in new colors. In reality, I'd just lost my virginity in what was by definition a date rape. But in my new, improved version, I had just made love with the man I was going to marry.

I had myself so convinced of this that I walked home on cloud nine. Floating on air. Head over heels in love. I was sure Joey was "the one." I was so excited that I'd finally found the man who was going to make my dreams come true, the man I was going to spend the rest of my life with.

The most traumatic thing about that night for me wasn't even that I'd been raped; it was what happened the next day when I called Joey to say hello and to see how our "relationship" was going (remember, I was only fifteen). My dream guy was curt. Nothing like the night before. Joey immediately cut off my babbling and quietly said, "Please don't call me again."

Click.

The dial tone buzzed in my ear.

I was beyond devastated. I cried my heart out that day and for weeks afterward. I decided I hated Joey and I hated men. The rejection hurt me on such a deep level. It was another notch in the belt of abandonment that was squeezing the life out of me. It broke my confidence. It shattered my hope. It scarred my view of love.

Not long after the incident with Joey, I met a guy named Jeremy at a party. I walked into a room where a song by 2 Live Crew was blaring on the stereo. As I sipped beer and dangled a cigarette from my fingers, my eyes landed on a guy doing the "running man." I thought he looked ridiculous doing the dance; I'm sure he thought he looked pretty cool. I took my beer and cigarette to the other room and didn't see him again until a few weeks later.

We crossed paths off and on for a while, usually at parties clouded by lots of alcohol and a ton of pot. One time we climbed onto the roof of someone's house and talked about nothing and everything for hours. I thought he was a good-looking guy—he had a chiseled body, dreamy eyes, and a handsome face—but I still wasn't totally into him in the beginning. The more I got to know him, however, the deeper I fell. Before I knew it, Jeremy had become my life.

It was almost impossible for me not to fall madly in love with him. And it was equally impossible for anyone not to like him. He was a cool guy, adventurous and spontaneous. He'd pick me up and take me on long walks by the railroad tracks. We'd hitchhike to the city of London, an hour away, to get away from Stratford. I always felt safe with Jeremy, no matter where I was. He had a natural instinct to protect, though many times he took that impulse too far.

On the flip side, Jeremy and I were young and immature and didn't have much working in our favor. We both came from broken homes and didn't know how to love ourselves. As much as we tried, we would never be able to figure out how to love each other. We were doomed from the start.

Only a week after we started dating, Jeremy went away for his birthday. Somehow I found out that he had cheated on me while he was gone. I was livid, but he justified his actions by saying he didn't think we were in a committed relationship. It was an easy out. Then he offered a string of seemingly heartfelt apologies (a pattern I would soon grow accustomed to) and reassured me that he liked me a lot and wanted to be my boyfriend. I forgave him, just as I would many more times.

The cheating that happened during our on-again, off-again relationship wasn't all one-sided, though. I played my own part. I even betrayed Jeremy with one of his best friends. I was hurt and confused by our toxic relationship and felt compelled to get back at him.

Just as I had my own issues, Jeremy had his. I believe a lot of his demeaning and disrespectful attitude had deep roots in his own life. His dad was an alcoholic. Jeremy followed suit. By the time he was sixteen, he too had a drinking problem. I went to a few Alcoholics Anonymous meetings with him. We looked like babies in a sea of worn, tired faces that had lived at least twice as many years as we had. Jeremy didn't last long in the twelve-step program, and his drinking problem got worse.

There's no way to sugarcoat the truth: Jeremy was a jerk when he drank. I think he would agree with me on that today. He took on what I liked to call his evil alter ego, Jack (his middle name). Every word he spoke while under the influence was offensive and confrontational. Then there were the fights, most of which intensified when he had a few drinks in him. A natural born fighter (and a very good one, I'll add), Jeremy went to extremes when someone so much as looked at him the wrong way. It was worse when I was with him. We'd walk hand-in-hand down the street, and if a guy looked at me, even for half a second, he'd flip out. He'd grab me closer to him and possessively say, "Mine."

The majority of our on-again, off-again four-year relationship would be unhealthy, suffocated by mind games and distorted by insecurities. We danced to the tune of breaking up and getting back together so many times that a lot of those four years have smudged into each other. I can't even remember anymore when we were actually together and when we were on a "break."

At home, my fights with my mother continued, one after another. It didn't seem like there was any downtime, a time-out when we weren't at each other's throats. Finally, when I was sixteen and when Jeremy and I were "off again," I hit a breaking point. I decided to move out.

You'd think it would have been a big moment. I mean, I was still a minor. But I don't remember any drama surrounding my exit. Things had gotten so bad that I think when I left, my mom was more relieved than anything. She and Bruce could finally have a peaceful, calm, and quiet house. Frankly, they deserved that much. In retrospect, I'm sure my mother worried about me, though. How could she not?

While my mom and my stepdad regained a sense of normalcy at home, I moved in with three guys, one of whom I dated briefly. It was a stereotypical party house with people coming in and out all the time to party and get high. The place reeked of booze and stale cigarettes. The fridge was always empty except for beer and ketchup. The kitchen was a disaster—plastic garbage bags filled with empty bottles and pizza boxes littering the floor. But it was home, and there was nobody to yell at me and get me upset.

School wasn't a priority. I went every now and then, when I felt like it. When I did show up, I was stoned or drunk or both. When I didn't go, I was either sleeping or partying. The schedule was pretty consistent: Party at night until 6:00 a.m. Sleep all day. Party at night until 6:00 a.m. Sleep all day. I know, very inspiring.

I worked odd jobs to get money for rent and to fuel my drug habit. I worked the midnight shift as a cashier in a gas station for a while. As a night owl, I loved the hours.

All kinds of customers showed up in the wee hours of the morning—weary travelers breaking up a long trip, waitresses ending their day, cops starting theirs. I'd sit half-awake in the claustrophobic kiosk of the station that consisted of two tiny rooms and an even smaller washroom that could barely fit a toilet and sink. I spent my shifts swiping credit cards, giving change, selling cigarettes, and occasionally giving directions to a lost traveler.

Just before midnight one night, I started a shift as my best friend, who also worked there, ended hers. I washed my hands, mentally psyching myself up for the next eight hours. My friend, who was cashing out in the tiny adjoining room, droned on and on about the annoying customer who hit on her again. I laughed, secretly fantasizing that I was back in my warm bed, cozy and comfortable under the covers.

As I stood behind the sliding pane of glass in the kiosk, waiting for my first customer, a man entered the station wearing a dark ski mask. He pointed a gun directly at my face. "Open the door! Open the f—ing door now!" he yelled. My heart raced. I was paralyzed by fear, my eyes bulging out of my head like I was a cartoon character.

He motioned with his gun toward the kiosk door and thundered again, "Open the door!" From the corner of my eye, I could see another masked gunman by that door, impatiently waiting for me to unlock it.

Instead of obeying his instruction, I panicked. I let out a blood-curdling scream and dove headfirst for safety into the adjoining room where the cash was locked up. I think I scared him more than he scared me.

Preoccupied, my friend hadn't heard the raving gunman but was startled by my piercing scream and hard landing. "What's your problem?" she shrieked. She turned her head toward the direction I had just flown out of and saw the gunmen. As the guy by the door yelled at her to open it, she too panicked—and opened the door for him.

Both men shoved their way into the kiosk. One made his way toward me, his steel-toed boots heavily pounding on the floor. As he dragged me into the washroom, I could hear his buddy yell at my friend, "Put the money in the bag! And some cigarettes too!"

My gunman whipped out a long piece of rope and started wrapping it around my wrists. I sat on the floor in an awkward position. "Don't do anything stupid," he warned. Slamming the washroom door shut, he left me alone in the dark. I felt a mixture of fear and the chill of the toilet tank pressed against my face. I shivered, listening to the gunmen order my friend around and her whimpers to please not hurt her. I almost didn't believe what was happening. *Are they going to kill us? Rape us? Is this even real?*

Then as quickly as it began, the robbery ended. The men left with thousands of dollars and a pillowcase-sized bag full of cartons of cigarettes. Less than five minutes after the gunmen forced their way in, my best friend stumbled into the washroom to get me. Her hands shook like a bowl of jelly as she untied the rope around my wrists. We dialed the police and waited in fear, hoping to God that the gunmen wouldn't be back. It was the last day I'd ever work there. There was no way I was risking another robbery or something even worse.

Without the gas station job, my money quickly ran dry. Soon I found myself with empty pockets, trying to maintain a high party lifestyle and still pay rent. I had to figure out a way to make money somehow. Ironically, I began a small-potatoes scheme of stealing cigarettes from a low-end chain store. I'd walk in the store, grab a few cartons, hide them under my puffy Starter jacket, and walk out the front door. No one suspected me. My jacket was so huge, I could easily fit four cartons underneath that oversized thing. A pack of cigarettes cost about eight bucks back then, and I sold the entire ten-pack carton for twenty-five. It was a steal (pun intended), but it still didn't give me the kind of cash flow I needed to keep up my partying.

So I started dealing pot. Other people were doing it at school and making a ton of money. It was quick and easy, and because I looked so young and clean-cut, I was the most unsuspecting drug dealer you could find. I'd buy a few ounces of marijuana or hash and sell it in quarters, half-quarters, or grams, just enough to support my habit. I even sold hash oil too. It's a miracle I never got caught. I could have gone to jail.

As much trouble as I got into and as many bad habits as I formed in my youth, I can still say it could have been a lot worse. That sounds odd, doesn't it—calling a drinking, smoking, doping girl who stole and dealt drugs "not that bad"? But there were lines I wouldn't cross—lines I'm not sure would have been there without those seeds of faith that had been planted years earlier.

In the big picture, my consequences could have been a lot worse. I could have ended up robbing gas stations myself, or addicted to potent drugs like meth or crack. I'm certainly not trying to be the poster child for a recovering drug addict. I'm thankful I didn't have to go through the painful process of recovering from alcohol or chemical dependency.

I eventually moved back home after a few months on my own. The fighting between my mom and me picked up right where it left off without even a moment's pause. I feel terrible for what I put my mother through when I was a teenager. The anger and pain that had built up in me all those years leaked its venom on her. I didn't know how to deal with the wrestling match in my soul—hating myself one minute, yearning for love the next; full of rage one minute, indifferent the next. I cringe when I think about how rebellious I was at home, but it also makes me sad because it came from a place of agony. I always say those who are hardest to love need it the most.

Around the same time, I also fell back into my familiar pattern with Jeremy. We reignited our toxic relationship. Jeremy and I hung out a lot with our mutual friends, either partying or doing stupid things. One time, when I was almost seventeen, we were hanging out with our group of equally troublemaking friends. It was evening but still light outside, and like usual, we were broke and bored. We were loitering around the downtown area when we found an unlocked building. (Is it breaking and entering if the door is open?)

The empty warehouse was spacious and for the most part empty. We scattered around the perimeter of the room, nosily going through closets and cupboards to find, well, something. We found a bunch of yoga mats and dragged them to the open floor where we had a mini Olympic session complete with sloppy cartwheels and lopsided handsprings. Yeah, we weren't jocks.

After a while gymnastics got boring, so we started sneaking around the building. Still in the semi-dark, someone opened a massive cupboard that revealed a staircase. It was the strangest thing, finding a staircase in a cupboard. We starting imagining the horrible things we would find at the end of the stairs, until one of the guys dared another to be a man and check it out.

One tough guy accepted the challenge. He opened the door and slowly moved down a couple of steps farther and farther into total darkness, but then he freaked out and ran back up. Poor thing. He was teased mercilessly.

Another guy piped up at that point. With his chest puffed out he said with much confidence, "I'll do it." He didn't even make it halfway down the stairs before he too got spooked and ran back up.

I thought the whole thing was silly. I mean, seriously, what on earth could we possibly find down there? I straightened up all of my four-foot-six bad self, said, "This is a job for a real woman," and marched down the staircase. I groped my hand around on the wall, feeling for a light switch, and when I finally found one, I couldn't believe what I saw.

I gasped. When my voice echoed up the stairs, my friends started freaking out and ran away from the door. "No, wait!" I shouted. "You guys gotta come down here. This is awesome! You're not gonna believe this!" Though hesitant, my friends made their way down at my insistence.

"Whoa," someone said as they all reached the bottom and looked around. "This is unreal."

We all stood paralyzed with disbelief in the middle of a giant room that was the equivalent of a teenagers' playground. Video games, basketball hoops, a jukebox, and dartboards were all around us. It was like we found ourselves in a whole new world. Then it hit me. This must be the community center called the Bunker that I had read about in the local paper. We'd found it before it even opened. It was a proud moment for all of us.

For the next few hours, we were in heaven. The arcade games were open so you could put in a quarter, play a game, and get your money back to keep playing. We played game after game. We shot hoops. We blasted tunes on the jukebox. We played pool and Ping-Pong. And then we got bored.

I started investigating the place and noticed a booth in the corner that was locked. There had to be some money in there, or at least some snacks. As we huddled around the lock, trying to shake the thing open, we heard an indistinct noise on the other side of the building. We froze. Someone was there. Once we heard a door open and slam shut at an entrance other than where we had come in, we knew we had to get out of there. Fast. With our adrenaline pumping and nervous laughter, we booked it out of the building the same way we came in.

Because we found the place before opening day, we proudly hailed it as "ours." That seal of ownership was the only reason we ever came back. It was a Christian place, after all. There were Bible verses all over the walls and a cheesy sign that said, "No Drinking. No Smoking. No Swearing."

Right.

When the Bunker opened to the public, we were there every weekend. It gave us something to do and a place to go. We weren't totally innocent, though. We almost always brought beer in with us and hid it in back of the toilet tank to keep it cold. I got drunk at the Bunker more times than I'd like to admit. I even used to deal drugs there.

When I didn't feel like playing a video game or shooting pool, I'd hang out with John, the director of the center. I'll never forget the mullet hairstyle he wore for a long time, all business in the front and party in the back. It's still a running joke how during this time and for years afterward he looked like he was stuck in the 1980s. I'd always tell him, "Hey, John, the eighties called. They want their hair back." Despite his questionable choice of hairstyle, I found him so easy to talk to, and we had countless debates about life. He was caring and sincere, and no matter how hard I tried, I couldn't find an ulterior motive behind his goodness.

There was only one thing about him that bothered me. He talked about God. A lot. No matter what we talked about, he would always find a way to reroute the conversation back to God. It was annoying. But I let him ramble on and on about religious stuff because he was nice. And the truth was, I really liked him.

Even though John was kind to Jeremy, my friends, and me, he wasn't oblivious to what we were doing. If he caught us with beer or drugs, he kicked us out of the center immediately, although of course he always let us back in the next weekend.

John was the first person who gave me a chance. Who didn't dismiss me because I was young, stupid, or a troublemaker. John would also play matchmaker, pulling me toward a God who would forever change the course of my life.

One weekend in May of 1992, my friends and I celebrated May Two-Four (Victoria Day), a Canadian holiday celebrating Queen Victoria's birthday that for most partiers is a drunk-fest weekend. I partied hard. Jeremy and I had broken up a week earlier, right after I found out he had slept with one of my friends. The getaway was my escape—a chance to go camping, hang out with my friends, let loose, and leave my relationship drama at home.

I was wasted the entire weekend and ended up sleeping with a guy I was acquainted with. I wasn't a one-night-stand kind of girl. The stupid decision I made in my drunken stupor came from purely selfish reasons. I didn't have any feelings for him; I was just rebounding from my breakup with Jeremy and used the fooling around as an opportunity to get back at him. An eye for an eye, right?

A few days later, Jeremy called, and we performed the same old song and dance routine. He apologized for cheating on me and begged me to take him back. He was saying all the right things, all the things he knew could turn me into a deep pile of mush. "Baby, I love you." "Please come back to me." "I'll change." "I can't live without you." "We're so good for each other." "You're the only one I want." I was hopelessly defenseless against his cajolery. Of course I would do my part and take him back. I did every time.

I figured, though, that I needed to be honest with him about what had happened on my weekend away. Better to rekindle our relationship on the right footing rather than under false pretenses. My conscience wouldn't allow me to get back together with him without being honest.

Big mistake.

"If we're going to do this," I told Jeremy, "I have to tell you something." I paused, imagining his response. I knew he obviously wasn't going to react well. "I slept with someone last weekend."

Initially, my ugly confession was met with an unbearable silence from the receiving end of the telephone. It didn't take long, however, for chaos to break out. As I tried to choke back tears and pleaded with him to calm down, Jeremy went ballistic. All I could hear was pounding fists, heavy objects crashing, and glass shattering.

I felt terrible. Guilty and ashamed. Especially because his rage was sparked by a foolish choice I made. With the phone still nestled by my ear and the chaotic soundtrack of Jeremy's fit surrounding me, I got dizzy from all the emotions that swirled in my head.

Still, Jeremy flipping out wasn't something out of the ordinary. Neither was the long-winded tirade of insults he threw at me. And I knew at some point, he'd calm down. I'd say I was sorry a million times, he'd throw in a few more digs, and we'd eventually kiss and make up (only to do a repeat a few weeks later).

But this time things escalated to an all-time high. Jeremy lashed out with a threat to expose my darkest secrets—things I'd shared with him a few weeks earlier in a moment of vulnerability. I'd been certain that sharing the deepest parts of myself would bond us together. Never in a million years did I expect to have that confidence betrayed. But that was exactly what was happening.

In hindsight, I can see that everything Jeremy said came from a place of deep hurt. I had betrayed him, and he could not see further than a momentary reaction. His words were birthed from pure rage and irrationality, a destructive place both of us knew all too well.

I know all of that now. But in that moment all I could hear was a threat that cut to the deepest part of my core.

All I felt was darkness. Pure, utter darkness.

The phone dropped from my hand almost in slow motion and landed with a thud. Life as I knew it stopped. The world turned black. I couldn't breathe.

My hands started shaking in a fit of their own, and all I could hear was the gasps coming from my throat as I struggled for oxygen. As his words echoed in my head, a wave of shame drowned my logic, and in that moment all I could think was, *I have to die.* And it had to happen now.

In a matter of minutes, I closed the gap between wanting to die and trying to die. My brain was littered with a frenzy of next steps. I couldn't shoot myself because I couldn't get a gun in Canada. I wasn't sure how many and what kind of pills to take to get the job done. I was afraid of cutting my wrists because it'd take too long for me to bleed out. As I continued to eliminate suicide options to find the best one, I thought of my sister and how she was killed.

Bingo.

I walked outside the house and waited for the perfect opportunity. It had to be a truck. A big one. I didn't want to allow for any miscalculations. I'd time my death perfectly, I thought. I watched as cars whizzed by on my street. Chevy Impala? Too small. Ford Escort? Even smaller. Minivan? Getting there. Then I caught a glimpse of an oncoming box truck. Perfect.

Adrenaline pumped in my veins like a percussion solo. As the truck got closer, I hightailed it toward the street, running across our square front lawn and the cracked sidewalk where I used to play hopscotch. A few strides farther, and I catapulted off the curb directly into the truck's path. Midair, I could make out the face of the driver, who was turning white as a ghost.

I closed my eyes and expected to be pummeled to the ground by the moving weight of this massive vehicle. But nothing happened. The driver slammed on his brakes and adeptly maneuvered the skidding truck onto a side street right in front of my house. He missed. He was probably thanking God in that moment. I was cursing Him.

The screeching brakes pierced my ears. I was alive, with skinned knees and a few bruises to boot. I felt devastated and humiliated that I couldn't even end my own life. I saw the truck driver run toward me, sweat pouring down the sides of his face. Poor guy. I had given him the scare of his life.

"Are you all right?" he panted, out of breath and showing genuine concern.

I was speechless. Numb. I merely nodded in a dumbfounded haze and turned toward my house. My eyes were met by a fuming neighbor who had watched me attempt to kill myself. Even from a few yards away, I could see her glare at me as if I had just killed her best friend. I certainly didn't expect what came next.

She screamed obscenities at me from her porch and then came barreling in my direction, her eyes bulging with poison. When she got an arm's length away, she grabbed me, dragged me, and whipped me up onto my porch. As she cursed with indignation and called me terrible names, she spat with anger, "How could you do this? What were you thinking? How could you be so selfish?"

As I floated in and out of my thoughts, my neighbor continued her berating rant. Frankly, I didn't see the point. I had condemned myself enough. In fact, I was quite the expert at calling me names and putting me down. There was no need for extra reinforcements. No need for her to gut my heart like a fish. I did a fantastic job on my own, thank you very much. What I really needed in that moment was compassion.

The sting of shame and the suffocating grip of condemnation seared my heart. As I curled up in a fetal position, drowning out the neighbor's voice with my own thoughts, she finally threw her hands up in surrender. My stepbrother showed up on the porch, his eyes wide in shock, and my neighbor handed me off to him. Apparently, she had reached the point of hopeless frustration with me and pawned me off so Chuck could . . . what? Yell at me more?

Chuck led me inside the house and asked, "What happened? What made you do this?"

I had nothing to say. I didn't have an answer. The living room spun out of control and my mind was far away, far from the table in the corner, the old-fashioned couches, my stepbrother's face close to mine as he played detective to uncover the details of the last twenty minutes. He called my mom at some point. As we waited for her arrival, Chuck continued to hurl questions my way.

"Talk to me, Pattie. What got you to this point?" he asked again, determined to rouse an explanation out of my dazed stupor.

I couldn't respond. I was frozen. Trapped. I just sat at the kitchen table, stuffing my anger inside, and numbly stared out into space. I knew my mom would be home soon. What on earth would I say to her? As I sat on the cold, hard chair, I couldn't escape the gnawing feeling of wanting to die. It was all I could think about. The beckoning wasn't loud or intrusive, though. It didn't attack me with hysteria. It was hypnotic, softly whispering in my ear, *Die, Pattie. Just die.* The soothing lullaby consumed my thoughts until they became one with my spirit.

When my mom came home and sat at the table with me, her hands shaky as she tried to compose herself as much as possible, I opened up. I unleashed the truth of all I had suffered and told her about how I had been repeatedly abused for five years by those we both knew. I told her how I had agonized in shame and in secret for years. How Jeremy had threatened to tell. I told her I couldn't handle it. And I didn't know what to do with the pain.

I saw my mother soften a bit. And after we sat in silence for a few seconds, she made a shocking admission. "Stuff happened to me too, when I was young." She didn't say much after that. She didn't need to.

I don't think either one of us knew what to do at that point.

It was Mom who broke the silence. "I'm taking you to the hospital. We're going to get you help."

Six

I am troubled
I feel empty
I don't know what I want
Comfort, love and mostly attention
I have a wall built around my heart
I am worried
I am sad
And I'm filled with regret
Regret for not saying no
When I was little
When I was curious
And when I was hopeful

I wrote this poem on May 20, 1992, the day before I was admitted to Stratford General Hospital.

The evidence that I needed help was there all along. Silent cries. Acting out. Rebellion. All signs I was fighting for attention, for someone to stop and listen and tell me I mattered. Like so many others, I suffered in silence, unsure of how to claw my way out of the pit of despair and into light. The only way I knew how was to kill myself.

It hadn't been the first time I'd wanted to do so. Almost two years earlier to the day, I had written in my journal, "I'm so depressed lately. I'm always crying, and I've thought about suicide a couple of times but I doubt I'd ever get enough stupidness to do it." I guess I'd finally found the "stupidness."

Nothing happens overnight. I buckled under the combined pressures of the sexual abuse, deep childhood wounds, and simply being a teenager. The latter is hard enough. When you're a teenager, you are tangled in a web of hormonal mayhem. The roller coaster begins when puberty hits. So many things are happening. Mood swings show up. You're trying to figure out your identity on shaky ground. You get squashed in the frustrating place between being a child and being an adult.

Add to that whatever emotional and mental issues have followed you around since you were younger. If you don't resolve them, or at least work on digging out the roots of your problems, they just grow deeper. And you act out progressively worse as time goes on.

In this state it's easy to fall into abusing drugs and alcohol. It's how I numbed my pain. It also made my emotional condition worse and contributed to my severe mood swings. My highs were really high and my lows were extremely low. I was emotionally unstable, unable to find equilibrium. Being in a temperamental relationship didn't help matters.

I didn't protest my mom's suggestion of going to the hospital; a part of me felt I had to go. I was just embarrassed. A cloud of shame hung over my head, ready to burst. I knew where I would stay: the psych ward. The stigma of the "crazy" floor started whispering seductively in my ear.

You're crazy, Pattie.

Who's going to love you now?

What kind of girl finds herself in the crazy hospital?

When my mom signed the consent forms, the self-condemnation grew louder, making it almost impossible to convince myself that I wasn't crazy or stupid, that I was just a girl with a broken heart who needed some help. So I let go. I gave up. The last bit of faith and hope I'd clung to had been destroyed.

I was a patient for nineteen days, much longer than I would have guessed. I want to get one thing straight, though. The psych ward was nothing like it's often portrayed in the movies. The floor wasn't a human zoo overrun with patients soiling their pants and being chased by orderlies. I didn't see people in zombie-like trances aimlessly walking the hallways, talking to ghosts. And I didn't come across violent patients who needed to be contained in straitjackets to keep them from tearing up the TV room. The ward was actually quiet. And sad.

My roommate was there because she tried to kill herself by taking a bunch of pills. She seemed normal, friendly, and polite. Just like me. But if you paid enough attention to her beautiful face, you could make out a glaze over her distant eyes. I guess it's easy to recognize the look when you see it every day in the mirror.

I didn't think I was any different from the other patients—the depressed ones, the schizophrenics, the suicidal, the delusional. We had a bond; we were all troubled, just to different degrees and in different ways. Each of us was there to ultimately try to make sense out of our individual circumstances. Whether it was finding a reason to live or figuring out why we hated ourselves so much. Or trying to stop the voices in our head from controlling our thoughts. Or, like me, trying to get to the bottom of unmanageable and debilitating depression.

Why did I throw myself in front of a truck? Why did I keep returning to a volatile relationship that only dug me deeper into an emotional grave? Why did I think ending my life was better than living it? I had a slew of questions—some obvious, others unknown—that needed to be investigated. A big part of me was ready to dredge up the mess, to talk about my past and expose it to the light of day. But I didn't get to do that in the hospital.

My meeting with the admitting psychiatrist was unpleasant. He seemed cold and indifferent, flying through my mental health assessment as quickly as possible. Maybe he'd had a bad day and wanted to rush home in his fancy car so he could sit in front of a warm fireplace and nurse a glass of cognac.

He fired off each question in a machine-gun succession without taking any time to unpack each one.

"In the past two weeks, how often have you felt down, depressed, or hopeless?"

"How long have you had these feelings?"

"When did these feelings begin?"

I didn't expect the doctor to be my best friend and sit there for an hour patting my head and telling me everything was going to be okay. But I was put off that he didn't express even an iota of genuine interest. At least pretend! Look up from your notes more than for a fleeting glance. Give me a chance to answer the questions without being interrupted. Hey, I'm sure working in a psych ward isn't as fun as spending the day on a beach in the Caribbean. But still, a little effort goes a long way.

After an hour of asking questions, scribbling in his leather notebook, and constantly nodding like a life-size bobblehead doll, the doctor gave me some meds and left. I saw him maybe one or two more times before I was discharged.

I met with another therapist during my stay. Our meetings were pretty much more of the same. I was dying to talk about the sexual abuse in detail, not just as a passing thought when describing the symptoms of my depression. I didn't have much luck.

It would be like that for years. In the course of my search for healing, I visited with a number of counselors and tried different forms of therapy. I think each counselor assumed I had addressed my sexual abuse with the previous therapist, so the topic would never be broached in detail. The reality was, I had never combed through that part of my past. In a way, I felt I fell through the cracks, though I'm sure it wasn't intentional.

One therapist in particular, a sexual abuse specialist, was adamant that talking was futile. "You don't need to talk so much, Pattie," she told me. "Many people mistakenly believe that you have to talk about things to get better. That's just not true." Instead, she focused on a psychotherapy technique called EMDR (eye movement desensitization and reprocessing) that is used for people with PTSD. I had to think of a traumatic memory and focus on it while I followed her finger's movements and answered a few questions. I'm sure this therapy has helped others, but it didn't seem like it did a whole lot for me.

It wasn't until a few years ago that I finally had the opportunity to bring about lasting healing by dealing with the abuse. But back at the hospital as a teenager, I felt like none of my core issues were addressed. None of my hang-ups were discussed. None of the reasons I found myself in a psych ward, specifically the aftermath of the many years I had been sexually abused, were any more than merely mentioned in passing.

I was lonely in the hospital. There wasn't much to do outside of popping meds, watching TV, going to group therapy, and hanging out in the common area. I felt trapped, like I'd been given a prison sentence without the possibility of parole. None of the therapy seemed to be making a difference. Nothing in my mind or heart was being rewired. I was the same person with the same depressing thoughts, low self-esteem, and haunting past.

I didn't even get many visitors. Outside of my parents and John Brown, the director of the Bunker, I don't remember anyone stopping by. It was a sobering wake-up call that I had no real friends. Sure, I had plenty who would party with me in an instant, but when I hit rock bottom and acted out my exit plan, none of my party buddies showed up.

John, on the other hand, was determined to show me he was genuine and he really did care. He regularly visited with me. I always knew he was coming because I could smell him down the hallway. Well, not him exactly, but rather the unmistakable, mouthwatering aroma of the fast food he brought. John would walk into my room carrying greasy bags of McDonald's and KFC, and my eyes would immediately light up. Hey, what seventeen-year-old doesn't like junk food?

I didn't mind John's visits so much, even though he droned on and on about God. Though I was used to his constant God-babble from hanging out with him at the youth center, at times it grated on my nerves. *God this. God that.* As I half-listened while munching on french fries and fried chicken, I remember thinking, "This guy can't stop talking about God, and it's not even Sunday." Needless to say, he still left quite an impression.

The first time John came to visit, he brought a rose and told me that God told him to tell me He loved me and saw me like that rose— beautiful. I chewed on a Big Mac and stared at the perfect flower. First of all, I thought John was nuts for telling me he heard from God. Second, I thought he was completely off his rocker when God's message was that I was as beautiful as the flower John was holding.

Somehow I was able to get past the whole hearing-from-God bit. But I just couldn't escape the comparison to the rose. *Oh my gosh, there is no way I'm like that rose. I'm not beautiful. I'm not good. What planet is this guy on?* John continued to visit me and to share God's love for me in a caring way, but the more he talked, the more I thought he had gone bonkers. What did he know about God's love for me? Obviously not much.

One day he said something that struck me, something I couldn't even roll my eyes at in my head. "Pattie, when you hit rock bottom, you have nowhere to go but up. You don't want to live anyway, so why don't you just see what God can do with your life and what plans He has for you?"

With eyes of compassion John asked, "What do you have to lose?"

Though we'd had many heart-to-hearts about God, I'd never even entertained John's passionate belief that God loved me. I'd never experienced God before, let alone the kind of love John shared with me. Frankly, at that point in my life, I didn't know if I believed God even existed. I did, however, know pain. I knew abuse. I knew abandonment. I knew fear. I knew disappointment. I knew all the junk that led me to attempt suicide. But love? Not so much.

What do you have to lose?

The question stumped me. I had no defense. I was speechless because the truth was, John was right. I had nothing to lose. I had tried doing life my way and failed miserably.

After John left that day, his words echoed in my head. As I lay in bed, plagued by my life choices, by the path I had chosen, and by the injustices I had experienced as a child, I realized I really didn't have a better option.

I lay in my bed, mulling over what I was about to say. I felt vulnerable. Either I was about to pray to the God of the universe, or I would be talking to the ceiling, confirming my mental state as a deranged nut. "Um, God," I began. "If You're real, I pray You do what John said. Help me live my life. I don't know how to do this on my own." A part of me wondered what God could possibly do with my life. But I saw it as the ultimate challenge. I'd see what, if anything, He could do to redeem the story I had so poorly written myself. I was willing to give it a shot.

I knew there was more I had to say. I couldn't just stop there. John had talked to me before about how we are all sinners and how our sin separates us from God. He sent His Son, Jesus, to die for our sins so that if we accept His forgiveness, we will be reconciled to God. So I asked Jesus, "Would you forgive me of all my sins?"

The moment I uttered those words, vivid images flashed across my mind. I'm sure you've heard stories of how when people are on the brink of death, they see their lives flash before their eyes. Well, that's exactly like what happened to me, except the images I saw were specific and extremely hard to watch. Every sin, every wrong, every destructive behavior, every indulgence—everything I had done that was against what God desired for my life came to my mind. The sleeping around. The drugs. The drinking. The stealing. In that moment, I was made acutely aware of how sinful I was and how holy God is. It humbled me to the point where I couldn't see how God could even begin to forgive me. Maybe I had gone too far. Maybe I had crossed the line where His grace couldn't reach.

I felt so ashamed. And hopeless. I took my eyes off the ceiling, looked down at my hospital-issued slippers, and whispered, "If it's too late, God, I totally understand."

I spoke the truth. I considered the possibility that I was too far gone in my sin for God's forgiveness to reach. I didn't believe in or understand grace at that point. How could I? I didn't know a thing about it. How could I expect God to accept my apologies for living such a messed-up life and welcome me with open arms? It may have been too much to ask.

But then He showed up. God met me in such a powerful manner, there was no way I could doubt His existence or His presence anymore. Pardon the cheesy sounding details, but what I experienced next was very intense and very real.

With my eyes closed, I saw in my mind an image of my heart opening up. As it unfolded, gold dust was poured into the opening and filled every inch of my heart until there was no room left for even one more speck to squeeze through. Somehow deep in my spirit I knew the gold dust represented God's love; He was pouring His love into my heart. Then as quickly as it filled up, my heart closed and turned a blindingly bright white. I felt like I had been purified and cleansed from the inside out. I was in awe, and I was fully aware of God's presence.

But here's the thing: I didn't feel loved in an overly emotional or warm and fuzzy way. It was like a deep knowing. A love on a level I would have never before recognized. A love that could only come from God.

I started weeping. Tears of relief. Tears of hope. Tears of gratitude. Tears of myriad pent-up emotions, some of which I didn't understand. I felt like a woman who had been wandering in a desert for days without water and accidentally stumbled into a babbling brook. Still trying to wrap my brain around what had just happened, I sat in a daze, uttering in wide-eyed amazement,

"Oh my God . . . YOU are real."

"Oh my GOD . . . You ARE real."

"OH MY GOD . . . You are REAL!"

"Oh my God . . . You're really real!"

For the next few minutes, I sat unable to move. I was so over-whelmed by this knowing, all I could do was repeat that God was real.

I knew that if I was going to give God the reins to my life, there were certain things I would have to give up. If there was anything I understood about God from the little I had learned from John and my Catholic background, it was that God didn't approve of certain things. Mainly, the things I liked to do. I knew I had to give up some stuff. Stuff that I liked.

So believe it or not, I took a deep breath and gave God an ulti-matum. "God, if I have to give up my drugs and my alcohol, You'd better be better than them, because I like drinking and I like my drugs. But here's the thing: I'm not gonna play church. I'm not gonna be a pew warmer and be a pretend Christian or a hypocrite. So I'll give that stuff up, but You'd better be worth it." Maybe it wasn't the most reverent prayer, but it was honest. It was where my heart was. I've come to realize that God loves for us to be raw and real with Him.

I sat up and opened the drawer of the nightstand by my hospital bed. I reached in and found a Bible, a good ol' trusty Gideon Bible. Whether you're in a hospital or a motel, you'll always find one of these books keeping the drawer warm. Somehow I just knew I had to start reading the Bible. It was my first time, and I didn't exactly have a plan for where to start or how long to read; I just opened it up to a random page and started reading.

I didn't know a thing about the Bible. I certainly didn't know there were different versions of the book. The one I had in my hand was a King James Version, probably not the most reader-friendly for a newbie teenage believer. It was a black-and-white blur. All I could make out was "thee this" and "thou that," "art this" and "ye that." Every other word sounded like something from a foreign language or a Shakespearean play. I concluded God had a different way of speaking than normal people like me. "Okay, God," I piped up. "If I'm going to do this thing, You're going to have to teach me Your language."

I was so excited about what I had just experienced, I ran to the pay phone down the hall to call John. He was the only person I knew who would appreciate what I had just gone through. And maybe he could help me understand God's language. I thought about the many times he had talked to me about God and how what he shared had meant nothing to me. But after my encounter with God, everything John had said and tried to teach me came alive.

By the time I got to the phone and dialed John's number, I was out of breath from excitement. "You are not going to believe this," I blurted out.

"What's the matter?" He sounded concerned.

"Are you sitting down?"

"Yeah, sure, Pattie. What's wrong?" God only knows what John was thinking at this point.

"GOD IS REAL!" I practically shouted in his ear. I waited for John to react in a dramatic, almost disbelieving way. I expected him to say, "No way! C'mon! Get out of town!" After all, I thought I was telling him something he didn't already know, something that would turn his world upside down like it had mine. I knew John was a Christian, but I didn't think he knew the truth like I did. After all, *I* had just had an experience with God.

John laughed and was clearly enjoying the moment. I wasn't. I was getting irked. *I can't believe this! He's not getting it.* I tried again, repeating what I had just said, this time drawing out the words more. "GOD"—long pause—"IS REAL!"

"Yes, I know," John said patiently and by this point, I'm guessing, with a grin from ear to ear.

"No, no, no. You don't understand. I just had an experience. I'm not talking about the religion stuff you learn in church. I'm talking about the real deal." I continued passionately stating my case. "The God of the universe, the God who created you and me and the skies and the trees—John, that God is real!"

"Yes, I know. That's what I've been trying to tell you."

"Oh. Well, I just tried to read the Bible, but I can't understand it. It's full of thees and thous and says things like 'heretofore, inasmuch, wherewithal, notwithstanding.' And I don't understand a word of it. You're gonna have to teach me God's language."

"That's not God's language," John explained as he chuckled. "That's King James's language. The original Bible was written in Greek and Hebrew and later translated into English. So the King James Version is an Old English version."

John told me he'd be right over with a Bible I'd have an easier time reading. That evening in the hospital room, he prayed with me and read the Bible with me, a version in today's language I could understand.

John was so happy for me. And I am indebted to him because not only did he lead me to God, but he also discipled and fathered me spiritually. He taught me what it means to be a real Christian through the example he lived day in and day out. This wonderful man helped me to learn what God's love and grace is all about.

Before I was discharged from the hospital a week later, my doctors couldn't help but notice the change in my disposition. I carried on about my encounter with God and told them He was real.

They were skeptical. "So you're hearing voices now?" one of them asked me.

No, I wasn't hearing voices. I had met God. I had found a purpose. My life was redefined. The depression didn't weigh me down anymore. For the first time in my life, I felt free. I could think clearly. I felt a deep, indescribable love, a love that was the perfect fit for the ever-widening gap in my heart that nothing in the past had ever had the power to fill.

After I got out of the hospital, I was on a natural high for about a week, taking advantage of every opportunity to tell others that God was real. I talked to everyone—my friends, my family, the convenience store clerk, the mailman. Most of these conversations were one-sided, with me jabbering away nonstop to someone who was almost always politely smiling and nodding. I didn't realize at the time how irksome I sounded, but looking back now, I can certainly see it. I'm sure I annoyed some people like John used to annoy me with his God talk.

I can only imagine how I may have come across to some of my closest friends, telling them about God just after getting out of the psych ward of the hospital. Years later, however, those same people realized my change wasn't just a passing phase. They would even at times ask me for prayer.

In my defense, I was excited. I had just found out God was real, and I wanted other people—who, like me, had their doubts—to know what I knew. It was like what happens when you first fall in love. Flowers look more colorful. The sun seems brighter. Sunsets are more picturesque. I had that giddy, dizzying feeling, and I not only wanted the world to know about it, I wanted them to feel the same way. But no matter what I said, no one seemed to get it.

The fact is, I couldn't just give others my experience. It's like sitting down at a fancy restaurant and looking at a beautiful menu with vivid descriptions and pictures of mouthwatering dishes. You can't experience the deliciousness simply by reading about it, discussing it, and walking away. You have to taste it for yourself.

There may have been times I miscommunicated my faith or turned people off with my excitement. I've since learned how to be more sensitive to people and what they believe. I may not always see eye to eye with everyone, but I don't feel the need to have to convince them of my beliefs.

For a week after I got out of the hospital, I was euphoric. I had a sense of fulfillment and didn't feel the need to use drugs, alcohol, or even Jeremy to self-medicate, forget, or feel wanted. I had finally found what I didn't even know had been missing in my life. My mom didn't say much about my experience. She kind of brushed it off. One thing was certain, though—she was glad my partying ways were behind me.

Jeremy wasn't the biggest fan of my new faith; I think he felt threatened. He was jealous that all of a sudden, my focus was on

God instead of him. Jeremy didn't have the same power over me as he'd had before. And finally, for the first time, I could see how toxic and volatile our relationship was.

A few weeks after I left the hospital, Jeremy came over. He knocked on my door and begged me to come back to him. He looked like he hadn't slept in days. Dark circles shadowed his eyes, and his hollow cheeks aged him.

"Please, Pattie," he begged. "Just come back to me. Let's try this again. It'll work this time, I know it." His voice was so sad it broke my heart, but not enough for me to make another run at it.

I shook my head. "I can't, Jeremy. I'm sorry."

He asked if we could take a walk to get some air. He held my hand as he spoke. "Listen, Pattie, we belong together. We're meant to be. I can't live without you." I was quiet, unsure of what I wanted to say other than that I didn't want to get back together with him.

Jeremy still couldn't understand why I didn't want to take him back. It was out of character for me, and the whole thing puzzled him.

I was honest. "I'm finally happy, Jeremy. I have God. I feel free. And I finally realized I don't want to be in a poisonous relationship. It's bad for both of us."

Silence.

Jeremy nodded slowly, his eyes growing darker. I noticed the immediate shift in his mood. The calm broke. "This is what I think of your God, Pattie." He took a step back, loudly filling his throat with phlegm, and hawked a loogie next to my flip-flops.

Seven

My spiritual high naturally dissipated. At some point you've got to come out of the clouds and live real life. Again, it's just like falling in love. The feeling of euphoria is only temporary. It's cute not to be able to eat, sleep, or think about anything other than the person you have fallen madly and deeply in love with. But if that feeling continued at such an intense level, you'd never get anything done. You wouldn't be able to function. You wouldn't be able to work. You wouldn't be able to manage your day-to-day responsibilities. I couldn't live forever on feelings of ecstasy. I had to learn to balance the high with the realities of life.

Despite the fact that my life was forging a new path of hope, I still had a lot of internal issues that needed sorting and mending. The trauma I endured from my past sexual abuse and the consequential harmful thought patterns I developed weren't going to go away on their own or in an instant. Healing would come, but over time and in bits and pieces. That's not something I understood at first, and that lack of understanding is what allowed me to revisit the very things that had led me to my breaking point.

When I got out of the hospital, I started going to a nondenominational church that was different from what I had imagined church was like. Though no church is perfect and every congregation has its share of hypocrites, for the most part, I found the Christians at the church I attended to be very real and authentic, people who actually walked the walk and talked the talk. They led me by their example. They came from all sorts of different backgrounds and walks of life. And they taught me that Jesus is the foundation of the church—and the one who unites us all. We could respect each other's differences and learn from each other because we had Christ at the center of it all.

My hunger to know everything about my newfound faith was insatiable. For the next six months, I faithfully attended church every Sunday, sitting in the front row week after week. I went to Bible study. I was mentored by different leaders. I read books. I even called the pastors at all hours of the day and night (sorry about that, guys!) to ask questions and ask for prayer. I was a spiritual sponge.

The more knowledge I soaked up, the more I distanced myself from my partying friends. I didn't think I was better than them because my life was changing in a different way; we just didn't share much in common. I didn't want to spend nights and weekends getting blitzed out of my mind or carousing for guys. I wanted to clean up my act. I was heading in a different direction from my friends, and little by little the relationships I had formed, mainly through the common tie of partying and getting wasted, started fading away.

A few months after my encounter, though, I found myself frustrated because certain issues I struggled with weren't going away. I thought that after experiencing a second chance at life, I'd turn into a totally different person. I thought I would automatically be rid of bad habits, be less insecure, and have fewer hang-ups. I thought my not-so-healthy tendencies, my anger, and my bitterness would magically disappear. I thought I would turn into a Pollyanna who smiled all the time, was always positive, and never said a bad word (either out loud or in her mind).

I think many well-meaning Christians try to use Scripture as a Band-Aid to cover a gaping wound. Sometimes this leads to confusion, as it did with me. One of the Scriptures I wrestled with was 2 Corinthians 5:17: "Whoever is a believer in Christ is a new creation. The old way of living has disappeared. A new way of living has come into existence." I struggled with that because while I was spiritually new, the old way of living hadn't completely disappeared for me—I wasn't fully rid of all my bad habits, insecurities, and hang-ups.

I found myself fighting the urge to smoke and encumbered by heavy feelings of rejection and bouts of crippling anxiety. I had a tough time reconciling the old me and the new me. I didn't understand that I still needed a lot of healing. Healing that would take more time, therapy, and effort. Particularly more time. Without that understanding, I became more and more frustrated. I constantly beat myself up for not being perfect. I had to learn how to little by little "work out my salvation" (see Phil. 2:12).

The battle that raged in my heart showed up in my behavior, like the way I overreacted to things. I was on an emotional roller coaster, guarded one minute, incredibly sensitive the next. One day I'd want to talk to someone about my problems, and the next I'd want to be alone, purposely shutting out the people who loved me the most.

I also felt alone. While I was fortunate to have so many people in the church to love and teach me, they were much older. They had spouses and families of their own to take care of. I wanted—really I needed—to hang out with young people I could relate to and talk to about school, music, and your average teenage stuff. I needed friends my own age. In the absence of any spiritual peer support, I made a slow but deliberate detour. A few steps backward here and a few more there, and before I knew it, I was back at parties, drinking beers and smoking joints.

I was just looking for someone to relate to. That's all. I didn't intend to return to my old partying ways, though John had warned me it could happen. Though I promised him I wouldn't indulge while hanging out with my old friends—in fact, I swore that I would be a good influence on them—he knew better.

"Let me put it this way," he told me as he slid a chair out from his desk during one of our many mentoring meetings. "Stand on this chair."

I obliged.

John reached out his hand. "Now take my hand."

Almost immediately after I grabbed his hand, his strong grip pulled me down.

"Think about it. Is it easier for you to pull me up or for me to pull you down?"

Point taken.

But the telling analogy didn't stop me from visiting my old turf. It was awkward at first, being at parties completely sober. I felt out of place. Hanging out at parties when you're sober gets old quick. I started compromising a little here, a little there. One beer became a few, with long swigs from bottles of peppermint schnapps to boot. One drag became a joint, and all of a sudden dropping acid seemed like a good idea. Before I knew it, I was caught up in doing the very things I used to do to numb my pain.

I stopped going to church as often and had fewer conversations with John and other mentors at the church. While I didn't give up on God, the pull toward the past was too strong. The old bad habits, tendencies, and desires came back full force. Except this time I felt guilty. I couldn't escape that feeling. A year after I tried to kill myself, the peace and joy I'd once had was gone and replaced with waves of guilt. I was no dummy. I knew I wasn't living right. I knew I wasn't supposed to be doing the things I was doing.

I dangled between the past and my spiritual transformation and couldn't find equilibrium. I felt guilty around my old party buddies and guilty around church folk. Being in that middle ground for a while eventually dragged me down to the bottom.

I wanted to pray, but I had a hard time. Words didn't come easily. I didn't know what to say. Feeling too far removed from my faith, I made matters worse. I dug deeper into my old ways. Why not? I had already pushed the envelope. I drank more, I smoked more, and as the final straw, I reunited with Jeremy. I hung out with him and his friends on his birthday. He had one wish—me. I said yes.

Two weeks later, I was at the gynecologist's office. It was the last place I wanted to be. I could think of a thousand different things I would have rather been doing. Getting a root canal sounded better. I wouldn't have even minded being grounded. But lying spread-eagled on the crinkly paper–covered table as a male doctor performed an internal exam? Let's get this over with, and fast.

It was supposed to be a routine visit. Answer some questions, get poked and prodded, get asked if I had any questions, and schedule next year's visit. The internal exam took longer than I had expected. I watched the hands of the clock on the wall creep agonizingly forward as my mom sat in the corner, her face buried in a tabloid magazine.

The doctor snapped off his latex gloves, whipped them into a nearby trash can, and without missing a beat said, "Any chance you could be pregnant?"

My mom's magazine fell to the floor, the pages fluttering noisily about.

Are you kidding me?

The doctor asked me again, with the same casual beat he'd use to ask me if it was raining, "Is it possible you could be pregnant?"

I immediately glanced over to my mom, who sat in stunned silence, and loudly retorted, "No! Absolutely not! No way!" My face was beet red. I was embarrassed but also offended. How dare this doctor ask me if I'm pregnant in front of my mother! Couldn't he have pulled me aside? Asked my mother to leave the room? Called me the next day?

I sat up on the table and pulled my paper gown protectively around me. Pregnant? The doc must have been smoking something before he came to the office that morning. "There's no way I'm pregnant, doctor," I repeated resolutely.

"I don't know what to tell you, Pattie." The doctor shrugged. "From what I could tell, I'm pretty sure you are, so . . ." He started writing on a prescription pad. "I'm sending you to the clinic next door to get a pregnancy test." He ripped off the piece of paper and put it in my hand, annoyed.

My mother let out a muffled groan. "Dear God, Pattie, please don't tell me you're pregnant."

I rolled my eyes at both of them. "I'm not pregnant!"

I had been on birth control since I was fifteen, at my mother's recommendation. We were sitting at the kitchen table one day when she brought up the uncomfortable topic. "I think it's time for you to start taking the pill." I looked at her in disbelief. *What?* I was still a virgin. As a matter of fact, I had no plans to sleep with anyone just yet. That day, I felt my mom basically gave me permission to have sex. When I started taking the pill, I did so religiously, or so I thought. There was no way I was part of that 2 percent group of women who experience a "margin of error."

I wasn't pregnant. I couldn't be. It was impossible.

Nevertheless, my mother and I walked to the clinic next door. Neither of us said a word. My mom probably didn't see any point in questioning me again. We'd find out the truth in a matter of minutes. I stared at the cheesy posters on the wall in the waiting room. One told me to get checked for such-and-such disease. Another reminded me to eat more fruits and vegetables. The walls looked muddied. Dim and dirty. *Why am I here?* You can't imagine the temptation I felt to bolt.

"Pattie Mallette?" A nurse's head peeked through a half-open door into the room. "You can come in now."

My confidence was unsinkable. Doctor, nurse, whatever—no one was going to tell me I was pregnant.

After a urine test and a few more minutes of waiting, I stood in another room, having offered the only chair available to my mom. She probably needed it more than me. She was the one who looked like she was going to faint at any moment.

The door opened and the same nurse who had performed my test came in. She nodded sympathetically and said, "Pattie, the doctor was right. You are pregnant."

In the background I heard my mother say faintly, almost in a whisper, "Oh, Pattie." Her voice was soft, but the sentiment rang loud and clear—disappointment. Absolute and utter disappointment.

I almost lost it. *Lies, these are all lies.* I looked at the nurse like she needed to get her head examined. "No way. There is no way I'm pregnant. You're gonna have to do it again. The test is wrong."

The nurse repeated more firmly, "Pattie, you're pregnant. The test is 99.9 percent accurate."

I didn't budge. "Well, then there's still a chance I'm not pregnant. Do it again."

At my prompting, she did another test.

While waiting the second time, I started doubting myself. Though the denial was powerful, I entertained the maybes. Maybe not taking a pill on time. Maybe even missing one or two. When the nurse came back, she repeated her earlier diagnosis. I had no more wiggle room to deny the obvious. I was going to have a baby.

I was leaning against a wall when the nurse told me the results from the second test. I crumpled down to the ground like a rag doll. I was in shock, overwhelmed by the enormity of the situation. A baby? Now? The timing couldn't have been any worse.

I wasn't married. I wasn't old enough. I wasn't responsible. I was back sowing my old wild oats. A baby didn't fit anywhere in that picture. A baby didn't even belong near that picture.

I had nothing against children. I loved kids. I'd always wanted to have babies. But I had romantic hopes around that dream. I would have a husband. A handsome, supportive, loving husband. And a beautiful home. We'd be able to provide a stable environment for our kids so there'd be a minimum chance they'd have a messed-up life like mine.

But a baby in my life situation? It was a nightmare come true. Half praying, half crying, I sobbed, "Oh, God, no, no, no! What am I going to do?"

While my emotions ran the gamut at maximum volume, my mom was quiet. Though it was rough having her witness one of the most sobering wake-up calls in my life, I was glad she was there. It meant

I didn't have to uncomfortably break the news to her later. She comforted me as best as she could by reassuringly patting my shoulder.

I stumbled around for days, disoriented and still in shock. I couldn't process the logistics of the pregnancy—especially the fact that in less than nine months, I'd be the mother of a flesh and blood, living and breathing baby. It was a dream, right? And I was going to wake up real soon?

My mom also had difficulty with the news, but she had already determined a plan. Well, at least a plan of what was *not* going to happen. "I'm done raising kids," she told me in so many words. "If you choose to have this baby, you cannot live here." I'm not going to lie. I was bitter. Angry. Hurt. I felt rejected and abandoned all over again.

When my mother hinted that I'd be mainly on my own in this process, I couldn't afford to pretend anymore. I had to wake up and not only face uncertainty but also make the trek into the great unknown. Without the faintest clue how. And alone.

During my pregnancy I was strongly advised to abort the baby, but I refused. I was shocked by the amount of pressure I was getting to take that route. I had to fight for my right to keep the baby. Abortion wasn't an option I even considered. My decision was ironic considering that when I was on the high school debate team, I made many convincing arguments for a woman's right to choose. The only other alternative to keeping the baby was adoption, but I don't think I would have emotionally survived that decision. I wanted my baby.

After researching a bunch of pregnancy centers from the yellow pages, I found a home at the Salvation Army's Bethesda Centre in London, Ontario. When I toured their facilities, I knew in my heart that it was the place for me. I couldn't put my finger on it, but something about the place felt warm. It felt like home. And I decided it would be. It was where I would live, be educated, get counseling, and receive prenatal care and parenting training. My mom and Bruce didn't blink at my decision. I guess they figured if I was old enough to make a baby, I was old enough to figure out what to do about it.

There was one more thing I needed to do—tell Jeremy. I hadn't spoken to him in weeks. I thought of our baby and I thought of us as parents. Had a category been available, Jeremy and I could have easily been voted our high school's "Couple Most Likely to Not Succeed." We were young. We were foolish. We weren't ready to be parents.

I called him and told him we needed to talk in person. I have a feeling he knew why. It wasn't often I asked him for a face-to-face conversation. When we met, I was nervous, as one would expect. It was hard to look him in the eye. I hadn't a clue how he would react.

At first he didn't believe me, telling me the baby was probably some other guy's. After I gave him a few days to let the news sink in, though, he finally came around enough to take my word for it. I knew he was still partying at the time, so I was firm about what I expected if he wanted to go through this together. "I'm pregnant," I told him. "If we're going to make this work, that means we're both pregnant. And it means you're gonna have to choose between me and the baby or alcohol." I made my expectations clear. The drinking had to stop. The partying had to stop. The fighting had to stop.

That night Jeremy got trashed. The disease of alcoholism took first priority. I knew in my heart he had made his choice. I was on my own, and so was he. The next day I told him that actions spoke louder than words and I would be leaving for London. I made plans to start my new life at Bethesda by myself. I didn't need anyone. Not my parents and not Jeremy. I was on a mission to prove how capable and responsible I could be.

Eight

Emotions all twisted and hormones run wild
The weight of an adult, the fears of a child
Questions are racing, awaiting reply
Confusion sets in, I sit and I cry
I feel like I'm trapped in this nightmare I'm in
I feel like I'm losing, there's no way to win
My dreams have been broken, my plans
    rearranged
My attitude's different, my body has changed
I have to be careful of each move I make
And remember someone else's life is at stake
It's a lot to remember and a lot to go through
But somehow it's worth it to go on so blue
I'll find some more dreams and I'll make some
    new plans
'Cause I know I'll recover with my blood in
    my hands.

I was two months pregnant in the beginning of August 1993. Early on a summer morning, my mom and Bruce drove me to the Bethesda Centre, a large, nondescript brick building nestled in a quiet neighborhood off one of London's main city streets.

We pulled up to the front entrance. The tight knot in my belly unraveled. This was it. My new home. I felt anxious and uncertain.

After I unpacked from the car the few pieces of luggage I brought for my eight-month stay, my mom and I said our goodbyes. It wasn't a tearful parting, but that didn't come as a surprise. It didn't even bother me. I was bent on maintaining my independence from her. Even though I was petrified starting this new chapter in my life, I didn't let it show. There were no tears. No quivering lips. I wouldn't even let my eyes water. I maintained a strong and confident composure, pretending I was leaving for summer camp: *I'll be back before you know it, Mom. I won't forget to write and send pictures. I'll miss you. Bye.* But this certainly was no summer camp. I wouldn't return home having learned how to swim or ride a horse. I'd return with a baby.

I mastered a brave front while waving goodbye to my mom. When the car rolled down the small hill of a driveway and all I could see was fading taillights, the floodgates opened. Down tumbled tears of shame. Tears of remorse. Tears of fear. Tears for the unknown. As I gasped for air in the middle of a sob, I forced myself to calm down. All I wanted to do was check in and go to my room where I could be alone. I was engulfed by a sense of loneliness yet wanted to fester in those feelings by myself.

I picked up as many bags as I could carry and shuffled into the lobby. I looked around at the humbly furnished room. The linoleum floors shined and a few old paintings colored the drab walls. Through an open door in my immediate view, I could see a few teenage girls with rounded bellies sitting around a large square table making crafts. They were laughing, having fun. *I hope they like me.*

I was numb throughout the intake process. Most of it was a blur; I resorted to coping the best way I knew how—get through the hard part with as little emotion as possible. A sweet staff member led me to my room, talking the entire way about how wonderful the center was, how terrific the rest of the girls were, how much fun everybody was having, and how she just knew I was going to love it here.

I nodded and smiled, letting her run the verbal show. It kept me from having to let out as much as a peep. I was afraid if I had the chance to talk, I wouldn't be able to hold myself together. And I didn't want to collapse like a house of cards in front of a stranger. She'd probably just feel sorry for me and blame my emotional outburst on hormones.

Once I settled in and got comfortable, Bethesda ended up being a haven for me. I found a home where I'd had none. An acceptance I couldn't find elsewhere. The place had obvious idiosyncrasies, though. Just imagine what it's like living with ten pregnant teenagers. Hormones raging, emotions of different frequencies slamming into each other. One girl is upset at the world; another can't stand her changing body. One girl is scared of raising a baby alone; another can't stop crying at sappy commercials. We were emotional Gumbys, being stretched in all ways from the nonstop hormonal party in our bodies.

And then there were the cravings. This one wants ketchup chips for breakfast; that one can't say no to chocolate of any kind. This one can't stomach anything except ginger ale; that one lives on grilled cheese sandwiches. Some of us would even make runs to the local grocery store to pick up whatever we wanted so we could eat our hearts out.

We were a hodgepodge of scared, young moms-to-be. Bethesda was home to all kinds of girls—girls with a wild streak, girls who always made the honor roll, girls from broken homes, girls from rich families, girls who were recovering addicts, and girls who were goody-two-shoes. Though we came from different backgrounds, we had two things in common: we were young, and we were pregnant.

I appreciated the instant camaraderie. It was comforting to know I wasn't the only one treading unknown waters. Together we battled and shared our loneliness and our pain. We tried to encourage each other as much as possible. Some needed the support more than others. Like the girl who always cut herself. She'd lock herself in her room and slice her body with any sharp object she could find. I never knew how to help her.

There was plenty to do at the home. We didn't sit around all day watching TV and eating bonbons using our ever-growing bellies as a tabletop. Half of each day we had to go to school, which included basic classes we would have taken in high school like math, science, and English. We also took parenting classes. We had individual counseling sessions. We had devotions. We cleaned and helped to maintain the facilities. We would even get a little creative and put on fashion shows, parading our big bellies around.

Every once in a while different speakers would visit and talk to us about the realities of motherhood. They helped shoot down any romantic fantasies we had about parenting. So many kids think having a baby is like having a doll. You spend all day dressing them up in cute clothes. You cuddle with them and take them places where people fawn all over them. And of course they never cry. While some of those ideas may be true to a certain extent, there was a whole lot more to having a baby than most of us at Bethesda realized.

There's nothing cute or exciting about sleepless nights. Colic. The cost of diapers, wipes, and formula. Postpartum depression. The end—at least for a while—of going to movies and parties with your friends. The loneliness. The end of "me" and the beginning of "we." Never mind having to battle all of this on your own. In short, motherhood is a difficult journey. I'll never forget what one of the speakers told us: "Being a teen mom is no picnic. It's the hardest thing I've ever done in my life."

Something about what she said hit home. That day I determined that if I was going to keep my baby, I had to be prepared for the worst. No matter how hard it would be, I resolved, I would be the best mom I could be and give my baby one hundred percent of me.

Though I was determined I was going to be a good mom and had put my partying days behind, traces of my past would surface from time to time. It was one way I paid the price for the years I spent getting high. During my stay at Bethesda, I had several LSD flashbacks.

One night I abruptly woke up with a debilitating feeling of fear. It was the exact sense of paranoia I felt when I used to experiment with the drug. The fear enveloped me like a wet blanket, drowning me under crushing waves of anxiety. I felt like I couldn't breathe. I couldn't think. The fear settled heavily in my spirit and completely overwhelmed me. I freaked out, jumped out of bed, and staggered out of my room.

Somehow I ended up curled up in a ball under the pay phone in the hall. A night shift staff member was sitting at her desk. Without so much as looking up, she barked, "Go back to your room." What was she thinking? That I was on the ground because I was trying to sneak out? Maybe steal a cookie from the kitchen or have a late night gab session with one of the girls?

I didn't want to go back to my room. Aside from being yelled at, I felt safe being in the open. At the very least I could be seen and heard, maybe even helped. In my room I was alone. I could disappear in the paralyzing fear and no one would know. At least huddled under the pay phone, I had a chance.

The flashbacks happened a few more times. Each experience was different but lasted between fifteen and thirty minutes. The last one happened one evening when I was out to dinner with one of the girls. In between a sip of Coke and a bite of a juicy cheeseburger, the room started changing. It was another trip, minus the acid. The dining room spun in and out of different dimensions. I excused myself to the bathroom, trying to act as normal as possible, not letting on that I felt as if I was in another realm. Twenty minutes later, the world returned to normal (at least to my new normal), and I returned to the table. I'm so thankful that was the last flashback I ever had.

As much as Bethesda had going for it—and as good as it was for me—being there still wasn't always easy. I got homesick. And I wasn't always happy.

I didn't write much in my journal during this time. The few pages I scribbled focused on how miserable I was: "I'm so unhappy, but I play along to my friends and family. . . . I could sit in my room and cry for days, but I could also tear apart every f—ing thing in this place. Crying's safer, it keeps me out of trouble. I'd sure like to let some of this anger out, though. God help me."

It wasn't until I was more than halfway through my pregnancy that I knew my spiritual life needed a major adjustment. I still had not forgiven myself for taking steps backward. I was stuck in shame. Though I wanted out of the emotional quicksand where I stood, I couldn't move. John and his wife, Sue, kept me from sinking any deeper.

John visited with me a few times at Bethesda. I especially looked forward to seeing him; he always made me feel a lot better, less homesick. John and Sue were like second parents to me (and still are today). I loved this adorable, hippie-looking couple. I remember spending the night with them at their home once while I was pregnant. They prayed with me and actually tucked me into bed. It was such a sweet and intimate gesture. I felt so loved, so cared for. With her thick brown mane and dark, piercing eyes, Sue was beautiful inside and out. She showered me with affection and always encouraged me. John was a bottomless vat of fatherly advice; I always felt I could talk to him about anything.

One afternoon when I must have been seven or eight months along, John called and announced that he was picking me up for church that evening. He didn't give me a choice in the matter. "You can't say no," he told me. "I'm already on my way."

On one hand, I was reluctant. Church? I groaned. I hadn't been to church in months. I didn't want to listen to a sermon and feel more guilt or listen to some praise and worship music and feel unworthy to even sing along. I was more comfortable dog-paddling in luke-warm waters—not quite fed up with faith and ready to walk away but not fully vested either.

On the other hand, I was happy to get out of the center for a while, and the church John wanted me to visit wasn't our home church. I figured I'd feel more comfortable in the company of strangers than with people I knew. So I went.

Somewhere between the singing and the sermon, I confronted the choices I had made since my original attempt at allowing God to run my life. When I took my life back into my hands and started doing things my way, look where I ended up—pregnant, an unwed mom. If I truly believed God had a plan for my life, I wasn't going to get there by doing things my way. I knew I had to start living life God's way.

For a long time I had believed that God had rules just to have rules or as a means to control people. For instance, it was hard for me to wrap my mind around the "no sex before marriage" thing. If something felt right, how could it be wrong? Eventually I learned He has reasons for the guidelines He sets in place. They're not meant to keep us from having fun; they're created out of love, to protect and give us the best shot at being successful. God didn't want me to contract sexual diseases or get pregnant without marital support and stability for my baby or me. I finally started to understand the significance of Proverbs 3:5–6, "Trust in the Lord with all your heart and lean not on your own understanding; in all your ways submit to him, and he will make your paths straight" (NIV).

That night at church I had to figure out how to be transparent before God without being filled with guilt. I had to face God and I had to face myself. I knew I didn't deserve it, but I wanted another chance. I needed grace. Because so many of us lack grace for and from each other in our earthly relationships, believing in and welcoming grace from God almost seems impossible. But without an alternative, I accepted that gift even without fully understanding how far reaching God's grace is.

I recommitted myself to God that night. It took a lot for me to believe I could have a second chance, so praying for anything more was beyond the scope of my imagining. I didn't deserve anything else. But as I prayed, I thought about my baby. I begged God to at least, if nothing else, let him or her be healthy and have ten fingers and ten toes. In hindsight, I realize how ridiculously amazing God's grace and mercy is even in spite of me and some of the choices I'd made. Make no mistake, there are consequences for our actions, but sometimes God overrides even the very repercussions that should naturally come our way. He gave me so much more than I asked for.

With that prayer, I journeyed into the final stages of pregnancy. Life wasn't a fairy tale after that. I still had a lot to learn. Before I rerouted my life, my faith was genuine but immature. I lacked wisdom in a lot of areas. I wanted to live a life of faith, but I kept running into walls. The collisions slowly began to crack my thin spiritual bedrock.

I was easily moved by circumstances. It didn't take much to change my moods. When things were great, I believed that God loved me. When times got a little rough, I felt God didn't like me. I relied on my emotional state and what my circumstances looked like at the time instead of truth. But feelings are fickle. They come and go and change and then do it all over again. And life isn't always easy. Just because you go through hard times doesn't mean you're a bad person or you did something to deserve a crappy hand.

I still had my share of rough patches. I was at a youth event one evening and noticed that almost everyone in the room seemed to feel the presence of God. Everyone except me. In that moment, I felt like God was abandoning me. Like for whatever reason, I wasn't good enough for Him to connect with me in a powerful way. It didn't help that days earlier, I had felt a distance between God and me almost so wide that I wasn't sure if He was there or not.

Sensing my discouragement, the youth pastor pulled me aside and said, "Pattie, I feel like God wants you to hear this Scripture." He read to me Jeremiah 29:11: "'For I know the plans I have for you,' declares the LORD, 'plans to prosper you and not to harm you, plans to give you hope and a future'" (NIV).

I was polite. I smiled and said thank you. What I really felt like saying was, "Whatever." Don't get me wrong. It's a beautiful verse. It's powerful stuff. But at the time it sounded so contrived, like he was pulling a nice Bible passage out of his bag of tricks to try to make the depressed-looking teenage girl feel better.

The next day I went back to church, where we were hosting a guest ministry team. After the service I asked one of the leaders if she could pray with me. She started praying for me, then suddenly stopped.

"Wait right here," she told me as she ran to a pew to grab her Bible. She started noisily flipping through the pages until she found what she was looking for. "Pattie, I really feel God wants you to hear this verse." Wouldn't you know it, she started reading Jeremiah 29:11.

God got my attention with that, but only by a hair. *It's gotta be a coincidence*, I thought. *Maybe this is just a real popular verse, like John 3:16. Maybe Christians just love to quote it all the time.* When I got home from church, I checked my answering machine. A girl I knew had left me a message. "Sorry I missed you at church today, but I really feel God is telling me that you need to hear this verse. Here's what it says: '"For I know the plans I have for you," declares the LORD, "plans to prosper you and not to harm you, plans to give you hope and a future."'"

Really?

My palms started to sweat. I was beginning to believe that hearing this verse so many times was more than just a fluke. Was God trying to tell me something? Did He care for me? Did He love me? Was He really interested in my future?

I dialed a friend to share my experience. Though I was fully engaged in the conversation, I kept staring mindlessly at the calendar on the wall, not really paying attention to what I was seeing. As I listened to my friend talk, my eyes began to focus on the bottom of the calendar. I noticed the Scripture verse of the month. Guess what Bible verse it was.

For the next few days, everywhere I looked I saw Jeremiah 29:11. I saw the verse blazoned on a coffee mug I pulled out of the cupboard at a pool party and on the top of my daily devotional. A woman at Bible study handed out individual Bible verses to read, and wouldn't you know it, mine was Jeremiah 29:11.

I was blown away that God wasn't frustrated with me for not getting His point the first few times. He showed me how far out of His way He would go to get me to hear what He wanted to tell me—that He had a plan for my life. A good plan.

To help pass the time during my last few months at Bethesda, I wrote letters to my family and friends back home. It helped me stay connected, even though my friends couldn't understand or relate to what I was going through.

When I first moved to Bethesda, Jeremy and I were on one of our many breaks. Our relationship at that point was confusing. We kept in contact through writing letters and talking on the phone every now and then. He visited a couple of times.

On his last visit, Jeremy came by for a Lamaze class. I had asked him if he could come down once a week and take some birthing classes with me. Even if we weren't sure how to define our relationship, he could at least show support.

I walked into the Lamaze class with Jeremy, clinging my pillow to my side, feeling both anxious and scared. All the furniture in the room was pushed to one side. Gym mats and pillows dotted the floor, couples planted on the mats. Every girl had a partner, even if they weren't romantically involved. I couldn't help but notice the sweet intimacy that connected most of the couples. As I watched them whisper to one another in hushed tones and share private moments, I was jealous.

I knew Jeremy didn't want to be there. It was obvious. He didn't fit the bill of a healthy boyfriend, but I was still desperate for us to work out the kinks. We were having a baby together. We'd created a human being whom we would see for the first time in less than two months.

As the clock tick-tocked into the next minute, the instructor fiddled with the VCR, about to pop in a tape. Just as she cleared her throat and looked around the room, Jeremy squirmed on the mat. In a matter of a few seconds, he got up, looking visibly uncomfortable. Though he was physically present, Jeremy's heart wasn't anywhere near the class, our baby, or me.

"I have to go to the bathroom," was his excuse.

My heart sank. *Oh, God. It's happening.*

I wasn't stupid. *Please don't let him leave, Lord. Please make him stay. Please, God. I don't want to do this alone.* After Jeremy left the room, I got up as quickly as I could with my bowling ball of a stomach slowing me down. I caught up with him just as he was exiting the building. We stood near the door.

"I'm sorry." Jeremy put his hands on my shoulders and kissed my forehead. "I can't do this." With those stinging words, leaving behind fragments of the very emotions of abandonment, rejection, and betrayal that had hounded me all my life, Jeremy walked away.

I didn't even have time to protest. I couldn't move fast enough to grab him by the back of his shirt, pull him down, and make him stay. I couldn't reason with him or convince him not to leave and to instead support me and stand by me during one of the most trying seasons in my life. I was humiliated. Devastated. Ashamed. The room spun out of control. The air around me was still, silent. I could hear a pin drop. I stood in the empty hallway. Alone.

I didn't go back to that first class, and I didn't bother taking any others. I decided I would just wing it.

The day I went into labor, Jeremy was in the county jail for getting into a fight. I was a week overdue. My baby was pretty content staying in the womb. He took his time and didn't rush his appearance. (Ironic, considering once he made his grand entrance, he would constantly be on the go. His speeds have always been fast and faster.)

So a week past my due date, I went to the hospital to be induced. It wasn't the magical moment I had imagined since I was a little girl. I had pictured this moment with my husband, the father of my baby, clutching my hand by my side. I would have given everything just to have Jeremy there—whether we were together or not—supporting me, cheering me on, and celebrating the arrival of the baby we had created. I did, however, have support from others: my mom; my friend Missy; Jeremy's mother, Kate; and his sister, Bonnie. They all stayed by my side in the hospital room until I was taken into the delivery room.

There was no doubt in my mind: I wasn't going to play hero and try to give birth naturally. God bless the women who do, but I was totally fine telling the doctors, "I don't like pain. I'm a wimp. Give me drugs." Well, actually I simply yelled for someone to give me drugs for the pain. Now!

After the doctor broke my water, I immediately went into natural labor. I started dilating quickly, much to the doctor's surprise. Four hours later, I was ready to be wheeled into the delivery room. My mom came with me while Kate, Missy, and Bonnie waited anxiously in the waiting room.

After seven minutes of screaming and sweating, annoyed at the doctors and nurses who kept yelling at me to "push" (wasn't it obvious?), around one in the morning on Tuesday, March 1, 1994, at St. Joseph's Hospital in London, Ontario, Canada, I finally heard it . . .

The cutest little cry I have ever heard. Music to my ears. I kid you not, my precious baby boy sounded like he was singing.

The nurses wiped him off and laid him on my chest. My heart pounded. Was he healthy? Did he have ten fingers and ten toes? He was perfect. Seven pounds, fourteen ounces of squirmy, sweet perfection. I'd planned to call him Jesse, but when I saw my baby boy for the first time—when our eyes locked, the melodic crying faded to a whimper, and his tiny finger curled around mine—I realized he looked nothing like a Jesse.

"Hi, Justin," I whispered, wondering how on earth two troubled teenagers could have created the most breathtaking baby in the entire universe. I soaked in the glory of the most beautiful moment in my entire life, nestling my sweet baby against my skin. My mother beamed when she finally had the chance to hold Justin. She stared into his face, her eyes glowing with pride, with amazement, with gratitude. When it was Jeremy's mother's turn, she did much the same, fixing her eyes on her grandson with an intense awe. She gasped. "He looks exactly like Jeremy."

After all the visitors left and I found myself alone in the hospital with Justin, I finally had time to think. Something happens when babies are born. The world seems different, better. You care less about stupid things and you start thinking more about the future. Absent of a string of visitors, nurses coming in and out checking vital signs, and doctors following up, it was a taste of our coming life together. This was it. Justin and I were on our own. Something about his sweet, crinkly face and the adorable yawns where he resembled a baby lion tempered all the fears and questions that continuously tapped me on the shoulder.

> *How are you going to take care of this precious baby on your own?*
> One day at a time, I suppose.
> *Can you even afford a baby as a single mom?*
> I'll find a way.
> *What if he gets sick?*
> I guess we'll go to the doctor.
> *Where are you going to live?*
> I'll work out those details just like I worked out everything else.
> *What if? What if? What if?*

Who had the time or energy to get bogged down by the weight of those questions? I didn't. I had a baby boy to care for.

CHAPTER

Nine

Justin's hungry
My house is a mess
I don't have time for all this stress
It's one in the morning
So tired
So blessed
I think I'll go get some rest.

I stayed at Bethesda for a month after Justin was born. When I returned to the pregnancy home after the hospital, it was like a big celebration. I was exhausted but elated. The girls gathered around Justin, oohing and aahing, taking turns holding him and asking me about every detail of the birth.

I couldn't keep my eyes off the faces of those who were expecting in a few short weeks. Some of the girls, as soon as they nestled baby Justin in their arms, were enraptured by the heartwarming moment. I knew they were counting down the minutes until they would get to do the same with their own baby. They gently passed Justin on to the next eager girl, continuing to ooh and aah and badger me with questions.

Then there were one or two girls who looked nervous while sweetly cradling my barely-a-week-old baby. Anxious. It wouldn't be long before real life would kick in with an unstoppable force. I knew their emotions well—the torrid love affair between ecstasy and panic.

Eleven days after Justin was born, Jeremy was released from jail and saw our son for the first time. I was at my mom's house for a visit. As I sat at the kitchen table, cradling Justin in my arms and inhaling the scent of his newborn skin, I anxiously anticipated the knock on the door. I hadn't seen Jeremy since the day he left me at Lamaze class. Having Justin helped me push aside the bitterness I carried from that humiliating evening. The disappointment I had felt when Jeremy abandoned me paled in comparison to the indescribable love I felt for my son.

Still, I was nervous. I wasn't sure how Jeremy was going to react. Would he be excited? Would he be edgy? Would he be disinterested? As I tried to distract myself by focusing on Justin, I couldn't help but feel hopeful. I loved my ex. I always have. And I wondered if the minute Jeremy saw the beautiful masterpiece we had created together, he would find enough motivation to finally pull his life together and get his priorities straight. Maybe—and I hoped this wasn't just wishful thinking—we could even be a family.

Don't get me wrong. I was aware our relationship was toxic. I knew we both needed a lot of internal mending. I knew how bad things could be between us when they were bad. But even in light of those obvious and dismal realities, I couldn't ignore the glimmer of hope that whispered to me. Maybe, just maybe, Justin was the missing link to making our relationship work.

When Jeremy walked through the door and first laid eyes on our son, he simply stared. He couldn't stop. I don't think a herd of elephants dancing in the room could have stolen Jeremy's attention away from Justin. Awe colored his face. He was mesmerized by our little baby. As Jeremy wrapped his strong arms around this tiny swaddled creature, his stare melted into Justin's sweet face. There's not much I remember from that day except for the image of a man locking eyes with his baby boy with the kind of love that can only come from a father's heart.

I stayed at my mother's house for a few weeks after I left Bethesda and before I moved into my own apartment. She became my shopping buddy as I prepared for my new life. We scoured garage sales, secondhand stores, and other charity organizations collecting things for my new apartment. I was making a home for Justin and me. I was excited to have my own stuff and didn't care that the furniture I bought was once or even twice used. I wasn't bothered by the cigarette burns on the couches or that the kitchen table wobbled unless you stuffed rags underneath the legs. I appreciated everything I bought or received from generous and loving people and places like my church and Stratford House of Blessing, a nonprofit organization that provides living essentials like food, clothing, furniture, and baby supplies to families in need.

I was on mother's allowance, the Canadian equivalent of welfare, until I could support Justin and myself full-time. I didn't make much more than nine or ten thousand dollars a year, which included part-time jobs and social assistance. Justin and I didn't have much. It was a struggle to buy diapers and formula, but I managed to make it work. As poor as we were, my son never lacked for anything.

My mother and Bruce were amazing. They pitched in financially whenever they could. They also took care of Justin when I needed a breather. They often took Justin for a night over the weekend. When Justin got older, they contributed to his hockey fund, helping pay for equipment and uniforms, membership fees, and so on. I'll always be grateful for their help. I realize a lot of single moms don't have that kind of support from their own parents.

For the first two years of Justin's life, he and I lived in an apartment complex a few minutes away from my mom and Bruce. Our first-floor, two-bedroom apartment was small but cozy. It was just the two of us, so we didn't need much room. Outside of the questionable plumbing, the cheap aluminum window blinds that always bent, and the multiple areas of peeling paint throughout the apartment, it was perfect. It was home.

After I moved into my own apartment, Jeremy started coming around a lot. He was there so much, he started to leave things behind. A toothbrush. Some clothes. Toiletries. Spending the night turned into spending a weekend. Before too long he was living with us.

I never intentionally calculated on us being together. Sure, it was something I had secretly wanted, but only if his lifestyle changed. Looking back, I was so naïve. I allowed the relationship to progress by way of shutting my eyes and hoping that everything would magically work out between us. That we would be a happy family. An adoring, loving, functional family. Just like on TV. I never addressed the reality of what it meant for us to be together. As a matter of fact, we never even discussed us being together. It was an unaddressed assumption.

Though I had recommitted my life to God, I had still not committed my sexuality to Him just yet. Jeremy and I had been dating on and off for years, and I didn't know how to shift from being intimate with him to not. It would take time for me to address that part of my life. I was, however, still heavily involved in my church, attending Sunday services, youth group, and Bible study.

As weeks went by, the delusion that had blinded my good judgment started fading. It was obvious Jeremy had no intention of giving up his partying habits. He would stay out all night and sometimes even have his buddies over to the apartment to play cards and pound back some beers. The truth slapped me in the face like a bucket of ice water.

In the wee hours of one morning, I heard Justin wailing. He was up again for the umpteenth time. I could barely keep my eyes open from another night of only three often-interrupted hours of sleep. Jeremy wasn't even home yet. As I stumbled into our son's room, I knew at that moment I couldn't stay in a relationship with Jeremy. Not because I didn't love him, but because he wasn't ready to change. I was disappointed in myself. I was so stupid. Why hadn't I even talked with him about what it meant for us to be together—together as a couple and, more importantly, together as new parents?

I'd had it. The next morning I told Jeremy to move out. "I don't know what I was thinking," I admitted to him. "I'm sorry." We argued for a while and he left. I didn't hear from him for a couple of weeks.

The next time Jeremy called was the day I wondered if pigs really did fly. He was calling from rehab, where, he told me, he had found Jesus. And he wanted to talk to me about God.

His announcement was breaking news, but I was suspicious. I knew Jeremy. Was this a ploy to get me back? Time would tell.

Jeremy and I began spending every Sunday morning at church. We prayed regularly and even went to Bible study. I was amazed. Jeremy was not the same man he was when he skipped out on me during Lamaze class. This was a new and improved Jeremy, a man that I had hoped would one day exist. My guard started weakening a few weeks into his newfound faith. One Sunday in the middle of a church service, he asked me to go outside for a walk. Jeremy held my hand and looked pensive. He turned toward the sky and asked, "Why doesn't everyone know about God? How come they don't know how amazing He is?" It's one of the sweetest memories I have.

There wasn't a doubt in my mind that his transformation was authentic. His attitude and behavior were different than they had been in the weeks before. While our past was filled with futile promises of him changing, now it was actually and finally happening before my eyes. Jeremy was sweeter, more thoughtful, more kind and gentle. Best of all, he was more consistent than he had ever been.

So Jeremy was back in our lives and back in my apartment. He got rid of my secondhand couch and replaced it with an old one his mom had given him. Together we bought a beautiful wooden kitchen table with a built-in bench.

As first-time parents, Jeremy and I couldn't take our eyes off Justin. I melted at the slightest hint of a smile or a gurgling laugh. I loved how his tiny hands reached out for me, his mama. As I held Justin and pressed my nose against his sweet face, I disappeared into that distinct baby smell. He was a gift. He was entrusted to me. He was my life.

Our pastor eventually caught on to our living situation. (We never tried to hide it from anyone; we just didn't volunteer the information.) He pulled us aside after church one day and said, "We love you guys so much. We know you're living together, and since you already have a baby, I want to encourage you to think about getting married. It's the right thing to do."

Later that day Jeremy looked at me and asked, "So whaddya think? Wanna get married?" There was as much romantic sentiment in that casually thrown out question as in asking if I wanted a turkey sandwich. Still, I said yes. As unromantic as the proposal was, I wanted to marry Jeremy. We set the date for October 15, 1994, just a few short months later.

We went to a store to pick out a ring together. Since he never even officially proposed, he never got down on one knee and gave it to me. The engagement was nothing like I had dreamed about since I was a little girl.

When I was getting my wedding dress altered, I stared in the mirror. I imagined the walk down the aisle, and tears streamed down my face. I didn't foresee myself feeling cherished or special, the way I should feel on what was supposed to be one of the happiest days of my life.

We had a couple of premarital counseling sessions at our church. The counselors quickly came to the conclusion we weren't ready to commit to marriage. We didn't need them to tell us that. The evidence was blatant, though I didn't want to admit it. We were still so broken and hadn't dealt with all of our individual issues. So our relationship was never truly healthy.

Both Jeremy and I had a lot of living to do on our own before we could even think about committing to each other. But we didn't know it. I was desperate for us to work, and Jeremy was busy trying to work out his sobriety and his own issues.

I was also growing in my faith, but I had a lot of rough edges. It would take years to sand and soften some of them. It would also take time to curb some of my bad habits. I still had a lot of major changes to make. I struggled with smoking, and I had so much anger pent up from my past and in particular the years of sexual abuse. I ended up taking a lot of it out on Jeremy. I admit I was notorious for picking fights with him over some of the dumbest things.

The beginning of the end came one night when Jeremy was supposed to meet me at Bible study. An hour into the meeting, he still wasn't there. After the closing prayer, there was still no sign of my fiancé. I went home, put Justin to bed, and got ready for bed myself. Still no Jeremy.

Around midnight, I lay in bed flipping through the channels on TV, distracting myself from entertaining worst-case scenarios. Maybe he got into a car accident? Or something happened to his mom? In the middle of another infomercial for another useless product, I finally heard the front door open.

As soon as Jeremy walked into the bedroom, I could smell the booze.

"Where were you?" I asked, aware of the obvious. I was upset, but more so disappointed. He had done so well, staying sober for months. I was genuinely concerned. Why had he slipped up? "What happened, Jeremy?"

Jeremy was silent, taking his boots off and going through the motions of getting ready for bed. My disappointment quickly escalated to suspicion when he didn't respond to any of my questions. He was too quiet for his own good. I knew something was up and began to feel anxious.

I jumped to a conclusion. With sarcasm peppered with spite, I asked, "What? Did you cheat on me?"

Jeremy didn't say a word. The quieter he was, the louder the truth. I took my accusations a step further.

"What? After all this time, you cheat on me? Are you kidding me?" I jumped out of bed, ready for a knock-down, drag-out fight.

I finally blurted out, "So go ahead, tell me. What was her name?" I shot off name after name of girls we knew. He growled "No" after each one. Except for one particular name.

I said the name again. No response. Jeremy's silence said it all.

I was stunned. I knew for a fact he wasn't even attracted to and certainly didn't have feelings for this woman. "You cheated on me with *her*? You purposely sabotaged our family, your engagement with the mother of your child, with someone you don't even like?"

My head pounded. I sat on the edge of the bed swimming in emotions—sadness, anger, confusion. I stormed my way into the living room, taking deep breaths to calm myself down. Jeremy followed, trying to pull me closer to him with each step. He was finally able to grab me into his arms, his face pressed against my flushed cheek, rocking back and forth while holding on to me for dear life. The reality of the mistake began to make its way into Jeremy's heart. I tried to wiggle free as he poured out his apologies. Over and over the violins played while he told me how sorry he was and what a stupid thing he had done. "Please, please. I'm sorry, baby. I'm so sorry."

"I gotta go for a walk," I said, finally breaking free from his strong grip.

I ran out of the apartment to get some air, ignoring Jeremy's voice calling after me from the door. I don't remember if I put on a jacket. My heart was racing as I jogged down the sidewalk of the apartment complex. I was fuming. *How could he do this?* I passed one block. *And now of all times?* I ran past a few more. The release of energy was helpful, but it didn't push the elephant out of the room. What was I going to do? I needed to talk to someone, but who? I didn't have many friends.

I found a pay phone by a convenience store and called our babysitter, a girl just a few years younger than me (who a week later would end up sleeping with Jeremy). I vented for a few minutes while she patiently listened and consoled me. After I hung up the phone, I knew I still wasn't ready to go back home. There was one more person I had to call: the woman Jeremy had fooled around with that night.

The phone rang a few times before she picked up. I was calm. Cool. Collected. Ready to say . . . what? I hadn't a clue.

"Hello?"

When I heard the "other woman's" voice, the anger came rushing back. I verbally tore into her like a tornado ripping through a house made out of sticks. I called her every name in the book. "Do you feel good about yourself now?" I chided. "Do you feel like a winner? You destroyed every hope of happiness I had. You broke up a potential marriage. This wasn't just a casual relationship; we were engaged to be married. So thank you. I hope that makes you feel like a real woman."

She was quiet. I didn't give her much of a chance to respond. I continued my attack for the next minute or so. Then somehow, in an instant, the conversation turned. I started to feel bad about how I was treating this woman and how abusive my behavior was.

I took a deep breath and quieted my temper. I paused for another moment. "You might not be sorry," I began, calmer now. "But that doesn't matter. I'm going to choose to forgive you. I don't want to, but I know it's the right thing to do."

I hung up the phone following our exchange and walked some more. As the dazzling full moon lit my way, I thought about what I should do. Frankly, I didn't know. A part of me still wasn't ready to let go. Deep down in my heart, I wanted my relationship with Jeremy to work. I wanted to marry the father of my child. That was the way it was supposed to be, and that was what I wanted.

When I got back home, I told Jeremy we should take time apart to think. He didn't have a place to go, so I let him stay in my apartment. I packed a few things the next morning, and Justin and I went to spend a few weeks with my mom.

When Jeremy and I separated, we were deep into the planning stages for the wedding. The invitations were sent out. We had the flowers. I had bought my dress. We already had the money from our buck and doe (or stag and doe) party, a Canadian wedding tradition for an engaged couple. Invited guests purchase tickets to attend the nuptial fundraiser and enjoy a couple hours of drinking, eating, and playing games.

Even with all signs pointing toward the obvious end of the relationship, I wondered if there was any way Jeremy and I could salvage the wedding. I know. I was nuts. And blind. There's no other way around it; I was desperate. It's what kept me oblivious to the signs that screamed, "Run," "Leave," "Chalk up your losses and call it a day."

Almost a week later, while at my mom's house, I got a call a little after midnight. I knew it couldn't be good. No one called the house past ten o'clock.

"Hi," said the voice on the other end of the telephone. I recognized it immediately. Even from that sole syllable, I knew Jeremy had been drinking and his alter ego Jack had taken over.

"Hey," I said, still groggy from sleep.

Jeremy's speech sounded a bit slurred. "I just wanted you to know who I'm sleeping with in your bed." Pause. "Here she is."

A woman got on the phone sounding puzzled. I could tell she didn't know what Jeremy was up to. I recognized her voice too. It was a girl who'd been one of my best friends growing up.

I saw red. Rage ripped its way to the surface. I felt so betrayed. My heart was on its knees, begging me to do something, to end the insanity once and for all. I had tried to be the bigger, more mature person and had uprooted my life to let Jeremy stay in my apartment after he had just been unfaithful. And he had the audacity to cheat on me again, this time in my own home. In my very bed.

I dropped the phone to the ground, the echo of the dial tone bouncing off the walls. The anger finally shoved me into motion. *Go. Go. Go now!* I ran into my mom's bedroom. "Mom, I gotta go. Please, you gotta take me!"

She panicked, not knowing what was going on, and practically fell out of bed. Stumbling over her own feet while pulling on a pair of sweats, she stuttered, "What? Where? What's happening?"

I let it all out, telling her what had just happened. She didn't hesitate for a second. She pulled herself together and drove me to my apartment. I hopped out of the car before she even came to a complete stop. I booked it down the hallway, my legs spinning like an old-school cartoon character, and threw the apartment door wide open. This was *my* home. *Mine.*

The first thing I saw was Jeremy, two other guys, and my former best friend on the couch. Beer bottles were strewn all over the living room. They had been partying. I tried to stay calm. I swear I did. I tried to take a deep breath, but the anger had taken its toll.

"Get out of my house!" I yelled so loud the windows could have very well shattered. "All of you, get out!"

By this time my mom had caught up and stood behind me, ready to defend me if the situation required it. I was grateful she was there, even though I was so highly charged in that moment that I didn't realize she had come to protect me.

My former friend couldn't even look at me. Her eyes were glued to her shoes in embarrassment. She stood up along with the two guys. Meanwhile, Jeremy stayed firmly planted on the couch, crossing his legs and spreading his arms across the sides. He was claiming his territory. "Everyone sit down. No one is going anywhere," he barked.

The trio looked at each other and then switched glances from me to a smug-faced Jeremy. They slowly inched their way down to the couch, unsure of whether to stay put or get the heck out of my apartment.

"Get out," I repeated, my voice firm and threatening. "This is my home. My name is on the lease. Get out!"

They got up again, slowly, looking to Jeremy for direction.

"Stay put," he warned with a menacing look on his face.

I knew I couldn't fight this battle on my own. I picked up the nearby telephone and called the police. I said, "I have people in my house who won't leave. Can you please escort them out?" If I couldn't drag these fools out of my apartment, surely the men in blue could. I hung up the phone and threw Jeremy a satisfied grin. *How do you like them apples?*

He jumped off the couch and in one swift move got in my face and started mocking me. "Get out of my house. Get out of my house," he imitated with spite. We were nose to nose, so close—making it easy for one of us to do something really stupid. I decided I wasn't going to let him be the last man standing. As he continued to make fun of my threats, I smashed the beer bottle he was holding straight into his teeth.

My mom gasped. We were all shocked, Jeremy most of all. As he put his hand to his mouth, drops of blood fell and mingled with the beer on the floor.

Jeremy seethed. He started yelling and tossing vile obscenities at me. "You bleeping bleep bleep bleep!" Then he gathered a few things, summoned the three puppets with him, and walked out of the apartment.

I was so angry. A lot of my emotions were still built up from the last battle Jeremy and I had fought. Even though it was over, a part of me didn't want to give up the fight. I lunged forward and screamed out to Jeremy, "You—" My mother stepped in front of me, stopping me dead in my tracks. The door slammed and they were gone, leaving me to clean up the mess.

It was over. It was finally over. After four years of madness and heartbreak and confusion and stupidity and uncertainty, Jeremy and I called it quits for good. There would be no more apologies. No more running back into each other's arms. No more trying to make it work. No more vain attempts to piece together the brokenness. We were done.

I came back to my apartment the next day. It was practically empty. Jeremy had taken all the furniture out of the house, leaving Justin and me with just a television.

Ten

A few weeks passed before Jeremy and I spoke again. I finally got up the nerve to ask him if he wanted to spend some time with Justin. As angry as I still was, I didn't want to keep our son from his father.

When Jeremy came over for that visit, I noticed he hopped on my phone right before I walked out the door. As I said goodbye, he was distracted by the phone conversation and nodded absentmindedly in my direction. "See you, Pattie," he said and went right back to chatting with whomever he was talking to.

I returned two hours later. Jeremy was still on the phone. "Who are you talking to?" I asked, annoyed, wondering if he had been on the phone the entire time.

"My mom," he whispered without even looking up.

I couldn't believe it. His mom lived in British Columbia. It was a two-hour-plus long-distance phone call that I'd have to pay for.

I was furious. "Have you been talking to her this whole time?"

Jeremy stood up just as he hung up the phone. He cocked his hip to one side and spread his legs like a cowboy. His face was plastered with an all-too-familiar arrogance as he haughtily challenged my question. "Um, yeah, so what's it to you?"

I wanted to wipe the smugness right off his face. I couldn't stand his audacious attitude. I had no time for it anymore. I had depleted my reserve of patience, and in yet another display of immature anger, I lost my composure. With all my might, I swung back my right leg and kicked him where the sun don't shine.

Jeremy dropped to the floor, writhing in pain. He rolled around, moaning and trying to catch his breath. I'll be honest: it was pretty satisfying seeing him in a moment of weakness. It felt good to be in control for once. But I knew deep down that it wasn't the right thing to do. I also knew I could very well have just instigated a fight that had the potential to end badly, even in violence.

As my ex continued to groan muffled insults, fear gripped me. I started shaking. Though Jeremy had never been physically violent with me, I knew how strong he was and the temper he had. I knelt on the floor beside him and started apologizing. "I'm so sorry, Jay. I'm so sorry." He continued to roll around the floor in agony from my strategically placed kick. "Please don't hurt me," I begged. "Please don't hurt me."

I was petrified at that point. It was anyone's guess what would happen next.

Jeremy got up from the floor and in one move shoved me into the wall. I opened my eyes just as the spit from his mouth landed in my hair. Even though I hadn't moved, I was out of breath, panting for air that wasn't circulating fast enough.

My friend Missy, who had come back with me and had been in the other room, had run toward us. She bent down to pick up Justin as he crawled around the floor but froze when Jeremy yelled, "Don't you touch him!"

As I leaned against the wall, sobbing, Jeremy picked up Justin and started dressing him in his snowsuit. We begged him not to take the baby. We cried and pleaded, but he was determined. Missy and I knew neither one of us was a match for Jeremy.

Justin wailed from the chaos of the blowout while Jeremy struggled to zip up Justin's jacket. He suddenly stopped and put down the baby. He knew there was no reason to take Justin. Where would he go? What was he going to do with a baby? He didn't even have any diapers for him.

The reality of the situation finally exasperated Jeremy, and he left.

A few days later, after the adrenaline finally subsided, we were able to be civil enough to talk about Justin and make arrangements for Jeremy to see him again. Outside of discussing our son, though, there was nothing left to say. We barely spoke much after that.

I've often wondered why I stayed so long. Why was I so desperate for Jeremy and me to work out? I think it's simple—I was convinced there was a fairy tale that was reserved for me. A storybook ending that included a lifetime of love and happiness, an endless chorus of affirming words whispered in my ear by an adoring husband, and, of course, the standard-issue white picket fence.

I was always waiting for the moment when I would be loved and accepted beyond anything words or feelings could describe. And I thought Jeremy just might be the ticket to that fantasy. In a way, I was always optimistic—though you could argue naïve—that things would change. That he would see the light and love me the way I yearned to be loved. It was unfair of me to put so much expectation on Jeremy to meet all my unmet needs and fix all my brokenness. How could he? He was just as wounded as I was. And like me, he had no grid or reference for what a loving, nurturing relationship looked like.

It would take a long time, but eventually Jeremy and I got to the point where we maintained a healthy relationship. Though we've had our share of hurtful moments and on-and-off drama throughout the years, we've tried our best to keep our differences at bay. Today, I would even consider Jeremy a friend.

I once heard someone say, "It's not hard to be a single mom, but it is hard to be a good one." Single moms have to carry a heavy weight. It's lonely. Tiring. Nothing prepares you for being a mom, even if you have support. You can read (like I did) *What to Expect When You're Expecting* fifty times cover to cover. You can take a hundred parenting classes. You can listen to your mom, your friends, your neighbors, or the lady who does your hair talk until your ears fall off about their experiences. And you still won't be ready.

When you're on your own playing the roles of both parents and you walk out of the hospital carrying this wrinkly bundle of joy, you're even less prepared. And when you're not even out of your teen years, you just got thrown into a whole different game. It's tough trying to swing the bat with that curve ball thrown at you. The pressure can at times feel overwhelming.

I felt like I had to do it all. I had to provide for Justin's physical, emotional, financial, and developmental needs. I didn't have a husband I could hand him off to if I needed an hour break. I had to suck it up and figure it out on my own. And as small as it may seem, not having a partner was also hard for me because I had to lug everything around myself. Do you know how strategic (and strong) you have to be to carry a baby, a diaper bag, and a bag of groceries while manipulating a stroller?

Then there's discipline. I was in charge of setting limits, enforcing rules, and providing correction when necessary. It's hard enough to mesh different parenting styles when you're in a committed relationship; imagine how much harder it is to do when you're apart. At times my efforts to discipline Justin were thwarted because of how Jeremy handled him when he spent time with him. It wasn't always the case, but Jeremy admitted to me that he didn't want to spend the little time he had with Justin disciplining him and playing the "bad guy." I'm sure many parents feel the same way.

Unfortunately, it made my job a whole lot harder. I found myself having to be the bad guy while Jeremy was the fun parent or even the hero. The thing is, I've learned that children don't just *need* discipline and boundaries, they actually *want* those things. Even though kids may resist or challenge discipline, it creates in them a sense of love and security. And that's what I wanted for my son.

I survived single motherhood by sheer willpower and a ton of prayer. You do whatever you have to do. There really isn't much time for complaints or wallowing in self-pity when you're trying to change diapers, feed your baby, play detective to figure out why he's crying, find ways to come up with money for baby stuff on top of rent and utilities, and get educated to create a better future for you and your little one.

Like most single mothers, I quickly discovered the art of survival mode. It's not that I became numb in the process; it's just that sometimes switching on autopilot is the only way to persevere. It's what I needed to do to get through Justin's early years. If I was tired from being up all night and had to work all day, I'd drink an extra cup of coffee. If I came home from work after a stressful day and realized rent was due in a few days, I'd figure out a way to find the money. If I felt lonely when I saw couples together with their child at the park, at the movies, or at the mall, I'd pull myself together and try not to let that heartbreak rub off on my baby. I came to accept that life isn't always fair. That good things don't always happen to good people. And that no one is immune to tough times.

Jeremy and I had our rough patches in the beginning of our son's life. There were times he would make plans to see two-year-old Justin and not show up. My heart would break as I watched Justin sit on the front steps for hours, waiting for his daddy. I had to fight back the tears when I'd hear Justin ask with such longing, "Is he coming now, Mommy?" and then again an hour later, "Is Daddy coming soon, Mommy?" I'd always make excuses and pretend something had come up, reassuring Justin over and over that Daddy still loved him. "He'll see you next time," I'd promise.

I finally told Jeremy he had to stop disappointing his son this way. "If you don't show up one more time without at least calling to cancel, I can't allow you to see Justin anymore. It's your choice. You can break his heart this way once but not over and over again." I warned Jeremy not to call my bluff because I would keep good on my promise. Sadly, he did. A few days later, Jeremy was scheduled for a visit. Once again, he didn't show, nor did he call. I put an end to his visits.

Frankly, I questioned my choice. I knew what it was like to grow up without a dad. Though I was sure it was the right thing to do, the only way I knew how to stop the cycle of crushing disappointment, it still broke my heart not to allow Jeremy to see his son. That's why when he showed up two years later at church on Father's Day and asked for another chance, I was hopeful. I so desperately wanted Justin to have a healthy dad around. I wanted my son to have what I didn't have. Jeremy made a promise that he would never again break plans to see Justin without calling. To this day, he has kept his word. He has always shown up when promised.

(Although it took a long time for Jeremy to be present in Justin's life on a consistent basis, Jeremy didn't just show up when Justin became famous, contrary to what some media outlets have portrayed.)

While Jeremy was working on becoming a better father, we still had our share of drama. Whatever differences we had, however, we were intentional about not putting our son in the middle of our issues. We had both seen family members and friends use their children as pawns to hurt each other. We never wanted that to be the case in our relationship. So we always did our best not to bad-mouth each other in front of Justin, and we never withheld Justin from one another just because we were angry. We made sure Justin knew that both of us loved and cared for him, even though we weren't together.

Today, Jeremy is a totally different person than he was when Justin was a baby. He has changed in many ways for the better. Being a father is his first priority. It's evident in the way he is a full-time parent to his two younger children (from another relationship) and to Justin. I'm proud of what a great dad he has become.

When Justin was born, I hadn't finished high school. I knew I had to eventually go back and get my diploma. I wanted to; I just didn't have the money to pay someone to watch Justin while I was in school. Government assistance would pay for child care if I had a job, but they wouldn't cover it while I was getting an education. Their guidelines didn't make any sense. It was as if the government was trying to keep people from bettering themselves to ultimately get off the system.

My neighbor Mike would always remind me of the importance of education and encourage me to go back to school. He was a computer whiz. Mike came over one day to say hello. We chitchatted for a few minutes while one-year-old Justin crawled around on the floor, babbling away and playing with Mike's shoelaces.

"So, Pattie . . ."

I knew what was coming.

"You gotta go back to school," he sweetly reminded me as he always did. "You need your diploma."

We had a long discussion that afternoon about my dilemma and the ridiculousness of the system. While I complained, Mike listened and tried to be helpful. I didn't see him for a few weeks after we spoke.

You can imagine my surprise when I got a call from a local day care saying I needed to enroll Justin soon because someone had dropped off a check covering an entire year of day care. I almost dropped the phone. Who would do something like that? I knew my mom and Bruce couldn't afford it, and, well, I didn't know anybody who had the extra money to be so generous.

Somehow I found out it was Mike. When I thanked him, gushing my appreciation, he was bashful. His generosity was huge to me, but he didn't make too big of a deal out of it. As I thanked him and promised to pay him back, Mike interrupted my babbling gratitude. He had only one stipulation for giving me the money: "One day, help someone else go to school." In other words, pay it forward.

Mike told me someone had helped him when he struggled financially in college. Instead of paying back the money, he promised to down the road help someone else finish school. I am eternally grateful for his act of kindness. His generosity is nothing short of a blessing, a miracle.

I was surprised how much fun it was going back to school. I made a ton of friends quickly, an incentive to enjoy and not dread my classes. My friends and I had a blast, and I even maintain a few of those relationships to this day.

I was hesitant about going back to school at first, however. Unsure of what to expect. My life was radically different from the last time I had walked the halls. I didn't sit in class stoned this time. My mind wasn't a million miles away while teachers droned on and on about math or literature. This time I paid attention. I hung on every word. And after school, I studied hard while little Justin slept.

As a new mother, I had grown up. I was more mature than the other students. I worried about my future, about the well-being of my son, about creating a stable life where I could give him the best possible chance of being successful. Most high school kids don't need to think about stuff like that. They have partying on the brain. They spend their time playing video games, picking out cool outfits, or just hanging out. They're more interested in Friday night's football games than figuring out ways to pay the bills. And they should be carefree to a certain extent, not having to juggle responsibilities far above their maturity level.

Though my life situation was nothing like that of the typical high school student and some of the kids knew I had a baby, no one knew how old I was. Because I looked young and was young at heart, no one even questioned my age. It was assumed I was seventeen, just like everyone else. Except, of course, I wasn't. I was twenty. There were no extracurricular activities for me. No sports, dance recitals, or choir practices. As soon as the last bell of the day rang, I hurried to day care to pick up Justin.

That day care was such a gift. I appreciated that each day his teachers would write details about his day in a notebook. There aren't many earth-shattering things a one-year-old does in a matter of a few hours, but every now and then I'd read something that would make me smile . . . or shake my head.

For the most part, each day listed a different rendition of "Justin ate well" and "Justin took a great nap." Every now and then they noted Justin doing unusual things, like biting. I was embarrassed to read "Justin is biting his friends again" or "Justin did better with biting and only bit one boy." Other than that, though, my son was a pretty happy-go-lucky kid.

When I recently reread the notations in that notebook, I was blown away at how many of Justin's personality traits and quirks back then are still the same today. The teachers always (and I mean always) made notes of how energetic he was, how he was always on the "go-go-go," and how he loved saying "hi" to everyone he passed (Justin was a ham and loved the attention). As anyone who knows him today will attest, he is still very much energetic, busy, and friendly. Justin's love for music was also evident early on. His favorite time of the day was circle time, when the kids sang songs led by a teacher who played a keyboard. One entry especially cracked me up: "Justin's pants keep falling off, so we tied them with a string." Some things never change—I'm still telling Justin to pull up his pants, to no avail.

I can't begin to count the number of nights those first couple of years when I'd lie awake in the wee hours of the morning, tossing and turning from worry. Most times Justin would be up not long after to eat, so there was no point trying to get comfortable. I'd stare at the red numbers on the alarm clock, my body exhausted but my mind racing. So many questions cluttered my mind, weighing me down.

Will I be able to finish high school?

How many diapers does Justin have left?

How will I pay for day care next year?

Will I ever go to college?

On and on my mind would spin in never-ending circles. The worry was incessant, like a salesman who refuses to walk away until he seals the deal. I couldn't live wrapped up in a razor-sharp bundle of nerves. My head would have exploded. So I prayed.

Don't think for a minute, though, that I looked at God as a vending machine, where I'd pop in a prayer and out would come a miracle. I do believe God will come through for us when we pray; I just didn't expect Him to magically supply my needs while I sat back and watched TV all day or wasted the money I had on stupid things. From the day Justin was born, I was either in school, working, or looking for a job. My prayers were always birthed out of situations that were beyond my control, and the answers to prayer always seemed to come at the eleventh hour. Though I believed in miracles, doubt wasn't totally off my radar. And I won't lie: last-minute provisions aren't fun. They're frustrating.

Provision came in the craziest of ways. Random people at church, some of whom barely even knew me, would slip a check into my Bible when I wasn't looking. One time a group of ladies pulled up to my apartment and stocked my refrigerator and cupboards with groceries. Another time a man on a bus, a total stranger, walked up to me and said, "I really feel I am supposed to give this to you." He handed me an envelope full of cash, just enough money to cover my expenses that month.

Coincidence? Happenstance? Sheer luck? I don't believe that for a second.

The local food banks like House of Blessing greatly blessed Justin and me (as well as hundreds of other local families). We also benefited from the Salvation Army, which had programs where they would donate grocery store gift certificates to needy families. Those charities were lifelines for us. And today I'm proud of Justin for donating to various charities, including the ones that had helped us.

Financially giving back to God, or tithing, was important for me. Money is the only area in which God directly challenges us, in the Bible, to put Him to the test. "Bring one-tenth of your income into the storehouse so that there may be food in my house," He says. "Test me in this way. . . . See if I won't open the windows of heaven for you and flood you with blessings" (Mal. 3:10). So every Sunday, I gave ten percent of my income back to God. No matter how little I made. No matter how little I had left over.

A friend I'd known since we were five years old questioned my deep conviction. She knew me both before and after I was a Christian and had watched how I lived my life. She knew I gave to the church,

A *Journey*
through the YEARS

My mom with my dad

My mom, my dad,
Chris, and Sally

Early years . . .

Mom and Bruce on their wedding day

Still stealing kisses today

Our new family: Chuck, Candie, Chris, Mom, me, and Bruce

Full of smiles at five and six

Posing
with Bruce

At my sixth
birthday party

The house
I grew up in

Dressed up for
church with Robbie

With friends
on my ninth
birthday

Ready to perform
at the Stratford
Festival
at age ten

Growing up—love that '80s hair!

Expecting Justin

Walking the "runway"
at a Bethesda fashion
show

My mom with me
and a newborn
Justin

Bonnie and
Grandma Kate
with Justin at
the hospital

Father and son

With Grandpa George
and Grandma Kathy

With Grandma Kate

My mom and Bruce
with Justin

Four generations—
my mom,
my grandma,
Justin, and me

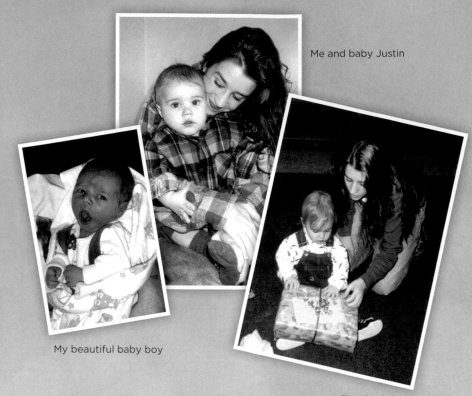

Me and baby Justin

My beautiful baby boy

First birthday

At the lake

Hanging out with his dad

A ham from the start

Snuggling with my boy

First day of public school

Justin's first love: sports

Fun times camping

Being goofy

Our first trip to Atlanta

In the cockpit

Scooter and Justin
clicked from the start

GROWING UP so fast . . .

but forever my
sweet BOY

and it was a difficult concept for her to comprehend. "Why do you do that?" she asked me many times. "Why do you give your money to the church when you can't afford it? I see your struggles. I know you don't have enough. If the God you believe in is real, why isn't He providing? Where is this provider of yours?"

I just smiled. "I'm not giving to the church," I said. "I'm giving to God and trusting in Him. God promises that He will multiply what I give. Watch what happens. Just wait and see."

Today, that same friend has seen what has happened since I accepted God's challenge. And it just about blows her mind. God has blessed me not only financially but in a whole host of ways.

You see, tithing isn't really about money. It's about being free from its control and trusting God will take care of you.

While Justin and I lived in that first apartment, John called one day and asked me for a favor. He had found a fourteen-year-old runaway named Liz on a park bench. She was homeless, cold, and hungry. He had talked to her for a while with one of his social worker friends. And though John wanted to help her out, he couldn't do much for her overnight. He wasn't in the business of taking home random teenage girls, so he asked for my help.

"Because I'm the director of the youth center, Sue and I can't take her home with us, but she needs a place to sleep," he said. "I'll figure out how we can help her tomorrow, but can she spend the night with you and Justin?"

John reassured me Liz wasn't a bad kid; she was just lost, literally and figuratively. Lost, hurt, and broken. He had a feeling the two of us would connect. Liz had a troublesome past and needed emotional safety. He hoped she would find it in me.

My heart jumped. Of course she could spend the night. Just imagining this young, helpless girl sleeping outside in an unfamiliar city broke my heart. God only knew what dangers lurked around and what kind of trouble she could get into. I told John to bring her right over.

I was surprised when Liz first walked through the door that night. She looked much younger than fourteen. Her strawberry blonde hair was pulled to the side in two neat ponytails, and freckles dotted her face. She didn't look directly in my eyes when she uttered a breathy "Hey." I knew she felt uncomfortable. I was a stranger, a stranger she had no reason to trust.

John was right, however. We instantly bonded. She was one of the sweetest, brightest girls I had ever met. The next morning I asked John if I could keep her. I was serious. Liz had nowhere to go. At the least I could provide her with a roof over her head.

I wasn't sure how the logistics would work out; I just figured they would. John thought my offer was sweet but didn't think it was possible. Who would allow a twenty-year-old single mother to take in a fourteen-year-old runaway? It was a ridiculous thought.

After a few weeks, though, John and I found out Liz had been in and out of so many foster homes that her social worker was at her wit's end. She was desperate to find a home for Liz where she'd stay put. At that point, I don't think they cared where she stayed. So one day I got a call from the exasperated social worker. "Here's the deal, Pattie. If Liz agrees to stay with you, we'll interview you, check out your apartment, and then make a decision." It was as simple as that.

When Liz moved in, we quickly discovered our apartment was too small. The addition of Liz to our household meant it was time to move. But how? Where? And, oh yeah, there was that little problem of money. I barely had anything left after using my assistance checks to pay for rent, utilities, and food. But I wasn't too worried. I gave my notice to the landlord. We couldn't stay much longer in an apartment where the three of us would literally bump into each other just about every time we moved.

I had two months to find a place I could afford. More than enough time, or so I thought. The waiting list for rent-geared-to-income housing was so long that we would need to look elsewhere. (By the time we got to the top of the list, Justin would already be in kindergarten.) I started looking for an apartment that would fit my measly budget. It wasn't the easiest house hunt. I searched in the paper, asked around, and browsed online. I prayed and I waited. Nothing.

At the end of every church service, I asked my friend Tim for prayer about my apartment search. We did the same thing each week: I'd ask for prayer and he'd pray. Sunday after Sunday, I prayed the same prayer with no resolution in sight. Three weeks before I was supposed to move out, anxiety set in. I prayed louder, stronger. Still nothing. A week later, I had a full-blown panic attack. Where would we live? It wasn't just me I was responsible for. I had to provide for a baby boy and a teenage girl!

Though he had watched my prayer go unanswered week after week, Tim didn't seem a bit discouraged or disappointed. He tried to settle my nerves. "I really believe God is going to teach you a lesson in faith through all this," he said.

I rolled my eyes at that. *Are you kidding me?* I looked at him, nowhere near convinced, and said, "If I'd just found an apartment, I could see how that could be true. But at this point, without even a potential place to live, this situation isn't giving me faith, it's weakening my faith."

He smiled. "Sometimes God makes you wait, Pattie. And then wait some more. And sometimes even right at the last minute, He makes you wait just a little bit longer until He comes through. It's how you learn to trust Him."

I wasn't so sure.

Another week passed. Nothing. I was beyond frustrated. Was this some sort of sick joke? Were we supposed to live out on the streets? Was that really what God wanted?

On the Wednesday before the three of us would be homeless, my mom called. She sounded excited. "There's a new listing in the paper for an apartment on Elizabeth Street, and it's available immediately."

Hope.

Finally.

I drove with Liz and Justin across town to talk to the landlord. By the time we arrived, one family had just finished a tour of the apartment. They looked like the perfect tenants—a strong-looking husband, a beautiful wife, and an adorable baby. I'm pretty sure I also saw a golden retriever with his head hanging out of the window of their minivan. And wouldn't you know it, after our tour of the place we saw another cute and perfect-looking family waiting for their appointment.

The three of us must have been quite a sight: a teenager dressed in funky clothes, a tired-looking mom who looked like a teenager herself, and a rambunctious two-year-old toddler. Oh well. We put on our biggest smiles and prayed the landlord would show us some favor.

The apartment was beautiful, complete with three bedrooms, a loft, an outside patio, and even a fireplace. The rent was cheap and included all the utilities. It seemed too good to be true. *Maybe it's a joke*, I thought as I walked carefully on the dark hardwood floors and grazed my fingers on the fresh coat of paint that adorned the walls. Doubt tried to weave its way into my heart. *Why would this guy rent to you? You guys look a mess! Why would he give this place to a single mom with a foster kid when he could rent it out to Mr., Mrs., and Baby Jones, a nice, normal family that doesn't have your kind of money problems?*

Valid points. Good questions. I couldn't answer them save for "I don't know." I don't know why this guy would choose us as tenants. I don't know why he wouldn't entertain other, better offers. I don't know. I don't know. I don't know.

But still . . .

After he finished showing us the lovely backyard where I knew Justin would love playing, the landlord spoke. "Listen. I could rent this apartment out to anyone. I've showed it to a lot of people, and I even have more appointments after you." He paused for a few seconds, carefully choosing his next words. "But I've been praying about who to rent this apartment to, and I believe I'm supposed to rent it to you."

I know it sounds far-fetched, but I promise you, it's true. That's when I realized that Tim was spot-on. The whole experience really did increase my faith. We lived in that beautiful apartment for almost three years. We were never late on our rent once, although we eventually got kicked out because it seemed Justin made too much noise. Between the drum playing, loud music, and typical toddler banging, we were a little too rowdy for our neighbors.

Liz stayed with us for a year and a half total. She was probably more of a gift to me than I was to her (though years later she wrote me a beautiful poem about how she was convinced I showed her the true meaning of love). Liz helped around the house and with Justin, who adored her. I like to think Justin and I were positive influences, because after moving in she stopped stealing and using drugs. She enrolled in school full-time and started going to church.

Although my life has been saturated with beautiful moments of miracles and provisions, like finding that amazing apartment, there were also moments of doubt, where the realities of life and unanswered questions distracted me in my heart.

Six years into my faith walk, I was taking a bath one night at a time when I was experiencing what some call a dark night of the soul. I had been begging God to help me with some things, but my situations remained unchanged. My prayers seemed to fall on deaf ears. I couldn't hear God in my spirit, nor could I feel Him around me.

I prayed. I cried. I begged. "God, where are You? I need You so badly and I can't find You."

My prayers seemed futile. I didn't know why I even bothered. Doubt began to leak its poison into me. I even started wondering if this whole faith thing was a big joke. Maybe when I lay in the hospital bed after I tried to kill myself, my wounds were so deep and my need so big that I merely imagined my encounter with God. Maybe I was so empty and lost that God was really only a figment of my imagination, a crutch I held on to so I wouldn't drown in my misery.

While I had run into other roadblocks in my faith, most of the time I could encourage myself or even be encouraged by others. There were times I couldn't hold on to my own faith, but I could hold on to the coattails of someone else's faith. On this occasion, however, I couldn't even do that. I didn't have the strength to ride out this storm by trying to grab hold of another person's life vest. So I was honest with God.

As I lay in the tub, I prayed. "I feel like I'm in a pit," I cried out, my words echoing against the bathroom walls. "I don't have the strength to hold on anymore. I don't see You. I don't feel You. This is goodbye." My prayer was honest, a cry from my heart. I was ready to throw in the towel. I was prepared to turn my back on faith and walk away. It had been a good run, but it wasn't for me.

That night I cried myself to sleep. I questioned everything. I mourned the end of something I believed in, something I had poured my heart into and had sacrificed the last six years of my life for. I had given up everything. I'd given up things I liked to do. And I'd done it all for a chance at having a relationship with a God who was not just the God of the universe but also known as a Father. That hurt the most. I felt like my heavenly Father had turned His back on me.

The next morning I got a phone call from a girl at church. We didn't know each other that well, but I liked her. "Pattie," she said, "I had a dream last night. It was about you." My breath quickened. I didn't want to jump ahead of myself, but . . . *could it be?*

She told me that in her dream she was walking with God in heaven and He was showing her all the marvelous things in that place. Streets of gold. Blindingly colorful fields of flowers. Choirs of angels singing beautiful melodies. Then He parted the clouds and looked down right at me. "Do you see my daughter Pattie?" He asked the girl. "I want you to go tell her I love her very much."

The girl looked at God, bewildered. "Why? I know Pattie. She knows You love her."

God shook His head. "No," He sighed. "She doesn't."

The girl was even more confused. "But I know about her relationship with You. Trust me, she knows."

God was adamant. "No, she doesn't. I need you to go to Pattie and tell her I love her. And also tell her I see that she's in a pit, and I'm going to be the one who lifts her out."

After the girl finished telling me about the dream, she encouraged me with this verse:

> He lifted me out of the pit of despair,
>   out of the mud and the mire.
> He set my feet on solid ground
>   and steadied me as I walked along.
> He has given me a new song to sing,
>   a hymn of praise to our God.
> Many will see what he has done and be amazed.
>   They will put their trust in the LORD. (Ps. 40:2–3 NLT)

In that moment, the weight of feeling like my faith was empty or futile was lifted. I cried tears of relief. The dreaded fear of being abandoned was gone. God hadn't left me. My faith wasn't a sick or twisted joke.

Yet again, God had gone out of His way to assure me He was present. I wasn't a forgotten child. He valued me. And I was worth enough for Him to take the time to make sure I got the message loud and clear.

Eleven

Growing up, my son was a combination of Curious George, Dennis the Menace, Zack Morris, and Bart Simpson rolled into one. Women I knew who had multiple children actually told me that just watching Justin wore them out. The kid couldn't sit still to save his life. Justin had so much energy, he was the literal embodiment of the phrase "bouncing off the walls." I'm not even joking. Justin actually bounced off walls. Full of life, he was born ready to brave the world with a mischievous grin on his face and rambunctious energy in his step.

Early on, I gave up the hope that Justin would be a cuddler. When he started being mobile, tumbling and rolling about, he wanted out of my arms so he could explore on his own. He was always seeking independence. He'd loosely hold on to my hand while reaching out with the other to see what exciting new adventures existed beyond my reach, even if it was only a few steps away. Sometimes this hunger for exploring got him into trouble.

The few times I could afford to buy some new clothes, Justin and I took trips to the mall. I'd browse through the circular clothing racks and play peekaboo with him. Pretending I didn't know where he was, I'd call his name while he hid and giggled loudly inside the clothing rack I sifted through. After a minute or two, I'd dramatically push aside a section of clothes, find him laughing hysterically inside of the rack, and yell "Peekaboo!" to his squealing delight. (How I miss those days!)

While I looked for a winter jacket on one such trip, two-year-old Justin and I engaged in our tenth round of peekaboo. This time, however, when I pushed aside the coats and yelled "Peekaboo," Justin was nowhere to be found. I panicked. I threw down the jackets I'd draped over my arm and dashed around the store, madly searching inside each clothing rack to find my little guy. He wasn't anywhere. Not in the rack of blouses. Not in the rack of jeans. Justin was nowhere in the store.

My heart pounded and my palms were thick with sweat. I hadn't been browsing at the rack for more than two minutes during our game; I didn't understand how he could disappear so fast. My heart pounded wildly in my chest. *Help! Where is my son?* I immediately alerted a store clerk, who helped me look for him. Maybe Justin somehow found his way to the back of the store? Five minutes passed and still no sign of him.

I ran out into the mall, calling Justin's name and asking passersby if they had seen a two-year-old blond-haired little boy wearing a red shirt and blue jeans. They hadn't, but they were kind enough to help me look for him. A security guard had run over to help me by that time and had radioed all the mall employees to keep an eye out for a missing two-year-old boy. Ten minutes had passed and Justin was still missing. It's a mother's worst nightmare. I was in hysterics, walking in and out of every store calling out "Justin! Justin! Justin!" I desperately hoped that at any minute he would turn the corner and run into my arms. But there was no sign of my son.

Finally, the security guard heard a buzz on his walkie-talkie. Someone had spotted Justin at the other side of the mall in the children's play area. I'd never run so fast in my life. I was panting and out of breath by the time I reached Justin. My lungs were about to explode. "Justin," I called out. My frantic heart was finally able to calm down at the sight of him safe and sound. My son, of course, hadn't the faintest clue I had spent the last ten minutes in an absolute frenzy trying to find him. "Look, Mom," he squealed when he saw me, without the slightest care in the world. He pointed to the rocket ship kiddie ride he was trying to climb. "Look, a wocket sip!"

Feeling equally relieved and irritated, I grabbed him. I hugged him so hard and so close, he tried to squirm his way out of my embrace. "Don't you ever do that again," I said sternly, wiping away the wisps of blond hair that were always covering part of his eyes. My voice softened. "Honey, don't you ever, ever, ever leave Mommy again." Finally able to wriggle free from my bear hug, he grinned from ear to ear and nodded his head. "Okay, Mommy! Can I pay on the wide now?"

Justin had a knack for pushing boundaries. The word *no* posed quite a challenge for him. Oh, he knew the meaning of the word, all right. He just loved testing me to see how much I really meant it. For instance, Justin knew the VCR was off-limits. He'd walk over to the table where it lay, put his hand a few inches above the VCR, and look straight at me. "No, Justin," I'd warn. "You can't touch that." He'd quickly yank back his hand, his eyes still fixed on mine.

Not but a few seconds later, he'd slowly reach his hand out again near the VCR. I'd repeat the warning. "No, Justin." Without blinking, he'd yank back his hand again. When he'd reach his hand toward the VCR for the third time as I said, "No, Justin," in an I-mean-business tone, he would pause for a second, look at me, then quickly reach out and pound crazily on the VCR with his hand. Then he'd hightail it toward the other side of the room, as far away from me as possible. He knew he was in deep trouble.

The thing is, Justin was such a cute kid, it was almost impossible to stay mad at him. By the time he was two years old, he'd already seen more than his share of time-outs. When I'd make him sit in a corner for whatever trouble he got into, sometimes Justin would turn around to face me, pouting his cherry lips and innocently blinking his big puppy dog eyes. He'd shrug his shoulders and raise his hands with his palms out. With toddler frustration, he'd whine, "Awww, come on, Mom! But I'm ohneee two!"

I was thoroughly amused every time and tried hard not to bust out laughing. "If you're old enough to know that, Justin, you're old enough to go in the corner," I'd say, doing my best not to smile. I never let on, but in those moments I'd want to scoop him up in my arms, hold him tight, and tickle him so hard his giggles would be heard in the apartment next door. But I knew I couldn't. Someone had to keep this force of nature in line.

When Justin was around three, I started homeschooling him, which I continued up until he was in first grade. It was an honor to be the one to teach him his very first lessons, the basics of which would carry him through life. I taught him how to read and write. Justin soaked up knowledge like a sponge. By the time he was four, he was reading full sentences on his own.

As a part of the curriculum, I taught him about the Bible and helped him put verses to memory. Friends and family would be amazed at how quickly Justin learned and especially how he could spout off a Bible verse verbatim when prompted by a chapter and verse reference. My son blew me away. He knew by heart at least fifty verses at one time and could recite them without missing a beat. It was impressive.

I loved homeschooling Justin and being his one and only teacher. If I could have afforded it, I would have done it his entire school career. Working part-time wouldn't pay the bills, however, so I had to enroll him in public school. Though I started him a year early and he had already completed the first-grade curriculum at home, I wanted to enroll him in a French school, so I let him repeat the year with kids his own age. While he was in school, I worked part-time at Zellers, a Canadian version of Walmart.

Justin got kicked out of his class the first day for making fart noises with his armpits. The teacher was well on in years, lacking patience, and couldn't handle Justin. She immediately switched him into a different first-grade class. She was the first of many teachers who would get fed up with my son. Justin wasn't purposely rebellious. He was a rascal in an unassuming, almost charming way. He sometimes got in trouble for things he didn't even realize were wrong. Like the time he was suspended from Catholic school.

Justin loved movies and would often repeat lines from them. When he was around seven years old, he watched a movie called *Good Burger*, which was based on one of the sketches on a Nickelodeon network show. In one of the film's scenes, a customer at a burger joint is complaining to Ed, a simpleton who works at the restaurant, about the hamburger he ordered. After his rant, the irate customer storms out of the place and yells over his shoulder to Ed, "See you in hell!" Ed responds good-naturedly, "Okay, see you there!" The scene was cute and funny, meant to make you laugh.

One afternoon when Justin rode the bus home from school, the Catholic bus driver wished him a good day as she let him off. Justin smiled, waved, and told her, "See you in hell, Bev!" He was suspended the next day. Justin wasn't trying to be mean, just funny. Unfortunately, the bus driver didn't appreciate my son's humor. He was always getting into trouble and pushing boundaries. It almost seemed like Justin would get suspended at least once a year for silly things like throwing snowballs or playing with bang snaps (the mini firecrackers you throw on the ground that make a popping sound).

A bright kid, Justin got bored easily. As he got older, I noticed his teachers either loved him or didn't. Some called him a leader. Others, who didn't know how to handle his contagious energy, were exasperated by his antics. All the kids in his class, however, gravitated toward him. I remember one teacher used to say that she had thirty kids and Justin. If Justin was happy and behaving, the other kids followed suit. If he was being a troublemaker, the other kids copied his behavior.

I remember one particular occasion when he got in trouble at school and was called down to the principal's office. Since it was such a common occurrence, Justin was prepared for his usual scolding. His teacher and the principal sat him down, but instead of yelling at him, they had a heart-to-heart with him. They encouraged him and talked to him about how he was a natural leader and what that actually meant. "Justin, the other kids in your class follow what you do and how you act," they explained. "So when you're good, they're good." These two people made such an impact on Justin. He came home from school that day beaming. "Mom, I'm a leader," he exclaimed, proud as a peacock.

I often use this example when I talk to parents of children with ADD or ADHD who get into a lot of trouble. While Justin wasn't formally diagnosed with either (though one doctor did comment he was definitely hyperactive), the signs were obvious. Justin was always distracted, he was creative, he was always doing several things at one time, and he couldn't sit still. I've learned that these unusually strong-willed kids are usually too smart for their own good. They're leaders in the making and need to be encouraged and shown how to redirect their energy appropriately. Children have different learning styles and should be taught according to how they learn. Unfortunately, most classrooms today aren't designed for that kind of individual instruction.

I've found great comfort knowing that many great leaders in politics, science, the arts, and the military had attention difficulties; some were even known for being troublemakers as children. I'll never forget a quote I heard in a video about a bunch of these greats: "Live long enough to irritate enough people to remember you."

I noticed Justin's musical talent very early on. It was hard not to; the boy had amazing rhythm. Even before he turned a year old, he could clap on beat to any song. When he was one, I'd bang out some beats and Justin would imitate me bang for bang as he sat in the high chair. He was a natural. He'd play the "drums" anywhere he found a flat surface: on pots and pans, chairs, countertops, the kitchen table, the bathroom sink—nothing was off-limits.

Justin got his musical abilities from both Jeremy and me. While I had grown up in the arts, singing and dancing, Jeremy's side of the family was also gifted. Kate, Jeremy's mom, was a very talented singer/songwriter, and others on her side of the family were also musically gifted. Grandma Kate made financial investments in Justin's music by regularly sending us money for drum lessons when he was younger. Jeremy too was involved with Justin's music. He always encouraged Justin and would also teach him songs on the piano.

So music was always a part of our lives. I had a lot of talented friends who would often come over for jam sessions. I loved to write and sing. My friend Jesse and I had many writing sessions at all hours. We actually sang at a couple of open mic sessions at a local hangout. One time we even had someone approach us and ask if we were looking for a manager. We laughed hysterically. No, we were just playing music for fun. We did, however, use Jesse's multitrack recorder to make home recordings of our songs (which I can't seem to find anywhere!).

At home, I'd sing and play on my keyboard, the used Yamaha I bought for $400 when I was ten. I purchased it using money I earned from acting in the Stratford Shakespeare Festival. Ironically, it was also the same keyboard I wrote about in my journal when I was fifteen. I was thinking of selling it for $300 so I could use the money to visit some cute guys I had just met. Thank God I didn't get rid of it.

When Justin was two years old, I bought him a mini drum kit. Without any lessons or directions, he picked up the sticks and started pounding away. He played for an hour. My friends and I watched in amazement as this pint-sized kid with tousled hair and half of his lunch splattered across his T-shirt kept a perfect steady beat. With his signature grin plastered on his face, Justin bopped his head up and down, keeping in time with the rhythm. He loved playing the drums so much, when he was four I got him a djembe, a goatskin-covered African drum that had a different type of sound.

By this time, Justin was playing complicated beats and could easily keep up during a jam session with my friends. He was so good at the drums that I took him for lessons. I'll never forget the first time I brought Justin to the music studio. We walked through the glass door into the classroom. A shiny drum set occupied one corner. The teacher, Lee Weber, had his back toward us as he shuffled paperwork on a desk in the opposite corner.

"Hi, Mr. Weber," I said. "Justin Bieber's here for his first lesson."

With his back still turned toward us, the teacher let us know he'd be with us in a minute. I hoped the minute wouldn't be longer than five. Sitting still and waiting? Definitely not Justin's forte.

Before we even had a chance to sit down, Justin made a beeline toward the drum set. "Justin!" I shouted, just as he hopped on the stool and grabbed a pair of drumsticks. Mr. Weber, still buried in paperwork, heard the commotion. Without looking up he assured us, "It's fine, Justin can play." I bet he was expecting to hear some little four-year-old kid bang away on the thing like a toy.

Justin started doing his thing. As he pounded out complex rhythms, he started attracting an audience. Students of different ages gathered around the open door, trying to get a peek at who was playing. When Justin banged his last beat, the teacher had already dropped whatever he was doing and was standing next to me. His mouth stretched to the floor in shock. The kids outside the door went wild. One of them squeaked to Mr. Weber, "That kid is amazing! If you're his drum teacher, I want you to give me lessons!"

Mr. Weber shook his head and lifted his hands in disbelief. "This is his first day. I haven't even given him a lesson yet. That's all him!"

After a few lessons from his first teacher, Justin went on to take lessons on and off for about six years from well-known local musicians including Wayne Brown and Mike Woods and a teacher we called "DLG." He got his first real drum kit when he was around nine. While Justin already had a hodgepodge of different drums we'd found at garage sales over the years, the young people around town were determined to give him a new drum set. They loved and believed in my son so much and wanted him to have an instrument that reflected his talent.

My good friends Nathan McKay and Leighton Soltys organized an all-day benefit concert in town, galvanizing local vendors, musical talent, and other entertainment to participate for free. People made whatever donation they could afford, and all the proceeds went toward Justin's drum set, a top-of-the-line Pearl full drum kit. There was so much money left over from the generous donations, the extra funds were put toward six months of drum lessons. It was a gesture (and a day) I'll never forget.

Justin was a visual learner. He'd watch someone play something and be able to instantly mimic his or her actions, whether they strummed the guitar or pounded out chords on a keyboard. And he played by ear. He could listen to a song and be able to play the exact melody and harmony and beat note for note. He soaked up music every Sunday at church during worship. The entire time the band played, Justin sat on the steps of the stage mesmerized by each band member. His eyes bounced from keyboard to drums to guitar, mentally recording the intricacies of each instrument and player as they produced beautiful and harmonic melodies.

Justin especially loved to experiment with different instruments. When my friends were over, Justin had a ball. Most times he kept the beat for us by playing his mini drum kit or the djembe. I always kept instruments around the apartment, given to us by friends, and Justin would fiddle around with them whenever he wanted. He was amazing at almost everything he tried. Justin even started writing songs as early as six years old.

Music was an outlet, a creative way for us to have fun and keep busy. While I encouraged Justin's natural talent, I never forced him into anything. I was proud of his talents and abilities, but I was careful not to pressure him to learn music. I always let him decide what he wanted to learn. If he wanted to play an instrument, I got him one. If he asked for lessons, I'd find the money to make it happen.

As good as he was at music, though, it wasn't his first love. There was one thing Justin loved more: sports. While music was a fun hobby, sports were his life. My little boy excelled at every sport he played. He practically skated before he learned how to walk. From the time he was five years old, he was on the all-star travel team for soccer and hockey each year. After he started playing sports, anytime I asked

145

Justin what he wanted to be when he grew up, his answer was always the same: "A professional hockey or soccer player."

Justin's love for music and sports was an interesting marriage. He was both athletic and artistic. One minute he was an aggressive and competitive center forward, dominating the ice, body checking and skating circles around his opponents. The next he was showcasing his natural talent as a musician with a natural charisma and ease.

My son was not just good at sports and music, though; he had a knack for doing so many different things well. Justin could skateboard, solve a Rubik's Cube in under two minutes, and even juggle. He won regional chess championships and junior golf tournaments. Pardon the proud mama moment, but I was fascinated by all Justin's talents. He was competitive, bright, and coordinated. The kid could do it all.

Investing my time in Justin's life was important, especially since I was a single parent. I had plenty of opportunities to work in a factory during the afternoons and evenings, but I never entertained the idea. I held down a few random part-time jobs, like Zellers, when Justin was in school so I could be home by the time he got there. Sure, I could have had a heftier paycheck had I worked the odd hours when Justin wasn't in school, but it wasn't worth it. I wouldn't sacrifice my time with him for any amount of money. Besides, I loved hanging out with him. He was my little buddy.

Faith was a big deal in our home. We went to church on Sundays and Bible study or youth group once a week. I even taught him in Sunday school. I prayed with Justin every night. We had a bedtime routine where I would tuck him in "as snug as a bug in a rug" and we'd pray together and talk about everything. There were times this fifteen-minute bonding session turned into hours. It was our quality time together. Our way of connecting. And we shared most of our laughs during this time. The nights we stretched our routine out, we would be delirious from fatigue and would giggle about the stupidest things. I cherish those memories. And Justin and I still talk about them to this day.

In 1997, Nations in Bloom named Stratford the prettiest city in the world. It's a fitting accolade considering the beautiful parks that adorn the city. Justin and I practically lived in Queens Park during the spring and summer months. We took long walks along the Avon River, admiring the old Victorian mansions that lined the waterway.

We chased each other up and down the stone pathways flanked by weeping willow trees and raced over picturesque footbridges. We fed the stunning white swans that dotted the lake. I watched Justin Rollerblade for the first time on the walking trails around the manicured gardens. When we were hungry, I set up picnic lunches on the tiny island just over one of the footbridges. Justin always begged me to venture out in the paddleboats, but I couldn't afford it. I would wistfully watch those boats and feel terrible I never had the extra money to give my boy a ride.

Two of the town's theaters were right in the park area, so when it was time for the annual Shakespeare Festival, Justin and I joined the massive crowds and people-watched. Because I had performed in this festival as a child, spending time there with Justin had a special place in my heart. It brought back memories. Good memories. Memories of when I dressed up in elaborate costumes and acted my heart out in front of thousands of people. Memories of me as a happy child in a happy place.

When Justin was around six and we moved to what would be our last apartment in Stratford, I was looking for a more permanent job to help support us. I asked my friend Mike (the guy who had paid for Justin's day care) for advice. Because I was pretty good at computers and was creative, he suggested I look into website design.

I wanted to go to a particular school, but I couldn't afford it. I heard about a government scholarship program that would pay my schooling costs if a company would guarantee me a job after I graduated. It was a catch-22. I had to find a job first, but no one would hire me without training. But I couldn't get training without having a job. It seemed an unlikely pursuit, so I put the scholarship program on the back burner and forgot all about it.

Because I still wasn't sure what specific area of the computer field I wanted to pursue, I decided to do some research. I was pretty determined. I cold-called a few local businesses just to get some information about their company and computers in general. I wasn't necessarily expecting a job. I was simply trying to open a few doors.

Using the same script every time, I called company after company. In a peppy voice I said, "Hi, my name is Pattie Mallette, and I'm interested in learning more about computers. Do you have a few minutes to answer a couple of questions I have about different computer careers?" Every phone call I made to all but one of the local businesses ended with, "No, I'm busy." *Click.*

My last call was to Blackcreek Technologies, a local consulting company that specialized in computer sales, networking, and custom solutions and also offered computer training. By that point, my expectations were pretty low. After I delivered my pitch, I was transferred to a man named Bill, the owner, who told me to come in the next day. I was in shock when I hung up the phone. It was a pleasant but certainly unexpected surprise.

When I met with Bill, he brought with him a website designer to answer specific questions. I was a bit nervous at first but peppered them with questions. I wanted to know everything I possibly could about computer careers to find a suitable match for me. I needed a good, stable, long-term job that could help provide for Justin and me. Whatever field would give me that stability would influence the kind of classes I would choose, whenever I could find the money to go to school. Somehow or another, I'd find a way to continue my education, even if I had to go into debt to do it.

To be honest, I didn't even consider asking Blackcreek for a job. It didn't even cross my mind because I simply didn't have any experience. I was just excited they gave me the opportunity to pick their brains, especially because after talking to Bill and his colleague (and mulling over Mike's advice), I decided to pursue website design.

A few days after my meeting at Blackcreek, I got a call from the woman in charge of the scholarship program. Imagine my surprise when she told me, "Blackcreek wants to help you out. They want to take part in the program and offer you a job." I felt so proud and honored. This was my chance to invest in my future.

In 2002, I graduated from Conestoga College with a degree in website design and joined the Blackcreek team. Outside of doing web design for the company and manning the front desk when necessary, I also subbed for the instructors in the computer classes they offered. If the company needed someone to teach basic computer courses like "Intro to Email" or basic Microsoft programs, I pitched in. I traveled to different schools, senior centers, and even people's homes for one-on-one consultations.

A couple years later when the company restructured, I was let go, but my superiors believed in me enough to invest in my future. They knew I wanted to start my own business doing website design and gave me a computer to help me on my way. Whenever they found themselves overworked and understaffed, they would also pass on their clients to me so I could expand my web design business and continue teaching computer courses. I was grateful for the support.

Though I worked full-time, I spent a lot of time with Justin when he came home from school. If I wasn't with him at soccer or hockey practices or games, we'd hang out on the ugly, old, yellow shag carpet in the living room and play board games or music.

We loved being spontaneous and taking road trips to nowhere. It was our special bond. We'd hop in my $700 boat of a car, an early 1980s Oldsmobile Cutlass Supreme, and take off on adventures. Driving down long stretches of highway with the windows down, we'd blast the stereo, constantly arguing about what station we should listen to. It was a power struggle, me setting the dial to a country station and Justin wailing in protest and switching it back to a pop one. We'd playfully battle it out between the likes of Faith Hill and Nelly.

There was only one genre of music we both agreed on—R&B. When I was pregnant and while Justin grew up, I listened to Boyz II Men all the time. Justin became a huge fan of the band. He listened

149

to Boyz II Men on repeat, memorizing every word and mimicking all the riffs and runs. Today Justin credits this band with inspiring him and teaching him how to sing.

We often took trips to visit my friends in Toronto, an hour and a half away. We loved walking around downtown and listening to the street musicians. On each trip we took, we had my friend Nathan accompany us. We didn't know the streets of Toronto as well as our hometown, and having Nathan around always made me feel safe.

I remember our first trip, when Justin was six. He took his djembe with him, ready to jam with one of my friends later that day. As we walked around the city, I couldn't stop staring at Justin's face. He lit up as he marveled at the sights and sounds of the city, the noisy mesh of car horns and buses and the hustle and bustle of people scurrying by. He looked up at the skyscrapers, astonished at how they towered over us.

He even got his first taste of playing in front of a crowd. We stopped to listen to a street musician. Justin sat down next to him for a few minutes and pounded away in perfect time on his djembe. He wasn't there long. But that tiny nibble was enough to make Justin want to come back to the city, just for the opportunity to play music on the streets.

Sure enough, not long after that first trip, Justin asked if we could take a trip to Toronto to play. Of course we could. We drove down to the city, picking up our never-ending tug-of-war about what we would listen to. As we walked around downtown, we noticed the *Speaker's Corner* booth in our coming path. It looked like an early version of a kiosk that sells subway or bus tickets. For only a few dollars, you could get a few minutes of recording time to rant, rave, sing, dance, or do pretty much whatever you wanted to do that was legal and not vulgar. The most entertaining videos were aired on the *Speaker's Corner* television show.

The booth attracted all sorts of people. Groups of friends who'd had one too many would stumble in front of the camera and slur their way through a sloppy take of "Sweet Caroline" or "The Gambler."

Environmentalists would plug the importance of recycling. Political activists would protest a bill that had been passed.

I had an idea. I asked Justin if he wanted to sing a song and play his djembe on camera for TV. He grinned from ear to ear. "Yes!" he answered enthusiastically. As soon as the distinct beep sounded signaling the camera was rolling, Justin started pounding away on the drum. He stared directly into the camera and sang along to the beats he banged out. "My name is Justin." *Ba dump bump bump.* "I'm six years old." *Ba dump bump bump.* Two minutes passed and people started gathering around on the sidewalk. They elbowed each other and whispered how amazing this little boy was. Justin barely noticed the attention; he was so focused.

After the camera stopped recording, Justin walked out of the booth and continued his mini concert in front of a growing audience. Having watched street musicians, he knew what to do. He whipped off his baseball cap and threw it on the pavement in front of him, continuing to sing and play.

I have to be honest: though he was entertaining and amusing, a part of me was embarrassed. Sure, busking was common practice on the streets of downtown Toronto, but people still had a somewhat negative view of it. Some viewed it as begging or panhandling, certainly not things any parent should teach or encourage their child to do. But I shrugged it off. I didn't care what people thought. Watching Justin go at it on the djembe made me smile. I simply enjoyed Justin's first time busking, the first of many to come.

I want to be clear. I never made Justin busk; he didn't even understand what busking was. He just wanted to entertain. And hey, if his playing inspired people to donate a few bucks, it was a bonus. I loved spending time with Justin this way because such a purity and innocence surrounded his playing. It was fun. He loved it. And I loved watching him. We giggled when he'd forget a word to a song. He'd encourage others who were watching him to sing along.

Justin wanted to busk all the time. While we couldn't take weekly trips to Toronto because I didn't have the extra gas money or the time, we spent many afternoons and nights in downtown Stratford, where the arts were welcomed with open arms. We loved going downtown. It's postcard worthy. Old World historic buildings mingle with modern boutiques and coffee shops. Looming over the city with its massive size and unique architecture, the courthouse is one of the most magnificent in the entire province.

The Avon Theatre, Justin's busking spot of choice, is nestled right in the heart of downtown and was always packed on weekends and weeknights. Locals and tourists watched performances like *Henry V* and *Romeo and Juliet.* Justin would sit on the theater steps strumming on a guitar that looked too big for him and singing his heart out. His sweet voice was powerful enough to reach adjoining blocks, making people curious about where the music was coming from. Like clockwork, crowds would quickly gather, and a seemingly endless stream of money would pour into the empty guitar case at his feet—piles of change, dollar bills, fives, sometimes even twenties.

I'd heard somewhere that busking without a license was illegal. I imagine because Justin was a little kid, nobody gave him a hard time. The Avon Theatre wasn't the only place Justin played. We'd scout out the regular busking hot spots, respecting the buskers who had already claimed their territory and moving on to find an empty spot on another block.

Some of the buskers had it in for Justin. In fact, one older musician, after discovering Justin playing in a location he frequented, got unnecessarily angry with my son. To punish Justin for "stealing" his spot, the old man grabbed a fistful of cash out of Justin's guitar case and took off running. Some guys in the crowd chased after him and caught him before he got away. They also gave him a very loud and very colorful reprimand for taking a little kid's money.

Because Justin was young (and extremely talented, of course), the crowd tended to be more generous with him than with the older buskers. People would toss ten- and even twenty-dollar bills Justin's way. He probably made thousands of dollars playing music on the streets. In one summer alone, he made enough money to buy us a vacation to Disney World. We had never before been on vacation, so when Justin suggested using his earnings to take that trip, I was flabbergasted. Of course I said yes!

I loved watching Justin perform. For about two hours, he'd sing all sorts of songs—worship songs, pop songs, and ones he made up days earlier or even on the spot. He was so confident, bellowing out tunes as if he'd been performing his whole life. It was fascinating watching a crowd of people mesmerized by my little boy. I was so proud.

Justin begged me to take more trips to Toronto, where he clutched his djembe and guitar as we roamed the streets. Justin was in his glory when he performed in front of random strangers. He had a playful energy that attracted people, young and old. Street musicians in their twenties would shake their heads at this miniature musical genius. They'd pass by with their tattered clothes and greasy hair and throw a few bills his way. Many times they would even give him their last dollar and in return make him promise to keep on playing his music and never give up.

One of my favorite memories is of one particular trip to Toronto when Justin was nine years old. We were walking around downtown, with our faithful escort Nathan, when something on a street corner caught Justin's eye. There on the sidewalk were two beat-up drum sets. A pail sat in the middle of the two instruments with two pair of drumsticks sticking out the top. A sign leaning against one of the tattered-looking bass drums proclaimed in bold black letters, "Pay $2 and play the drums with us!" Two twentysomething musicians were chatting with a passerby who had just thrown two bucks into the pail. When he started jamming with one of the musicians, Justin's eyes opened even wider. I knew what was coming.

When the jam session was over, Justin tugged at my arm. "Mom, can I play with them? Please? I'll even use my own money." How could I say no?

Justin practically threw down the guitar and djembe he had been carrying. He dumped two dollars in the bucket and picked up a pair of drumsticks. One of the musicians came over to him and tousled his hair. "How ya doin', little buddy?" I'm sure that just like Justin's first drum teacher, Lee Weber, he was expecting Justin to bang on the thing without rhyme or reason. The other musician stood a few feet away, puffing on a cigarette. Leaning against a lamppost, he smiled and waved to us.

Justin and the first guy hopped on their stools. Justin was chomping at the bit, drumsticks in hand, his feet tapping the concrete in anticipation.

"You ready, buddy?" the drummer called out. "Here we go. A one, a two, a one two three."

The guy started playing a rhythm. My son joined in on the offbeat, coloring the beats and complementing the rhythms. It was pretty impressive, another display of Justin's impeccable musical timing.

The drummer couldn't believe his ears. He shook his head in disbelief and whistled, "Holy smokes!" (except he used a more colorful word). He finally realized how good Justin was and started following his lead. The two of them jammed away, banging out contagious rhythms that you couldn't help but tap your feet to. The cacophony of the Toronto city streets was no match for these two drummers. It was like the entire block was on mute except for a little boy and a young musician battling it out on drum sets that had seen better days.

The other musician who had been taking a break started grooving. "Yeah, man," he yelled and slapped his thighs to the beat. Then he grabbed the empty pail and whipped a pair of drumsticks out of his back jeans pocket. Kneeling down on the pavement, he started banging on the plastic pail, complementing and adding a unique sound to the drums.

The three of them were amazing. Sticks were flying so fast they looked invisible. The passionate beats were flawless. The energy was palpable. It wasn't about a mere street performance anymore. The three musicians had surpassed showing off their skills to get a few bucks. The drums became extensions of their hands. Justin was engrossed in the rhythms. I looked at him and smiled. He was having the time of his life. This was Justin in his element.

As the sidewalk started swarming with passersby gathering around this musical trio, the energy grew. I stood shoulder to shoulder with people, barely able to move. People started grooving, bobbing their heads in time with the music. No one looked hurried, a strange sight in a big city. It was as if everyone had all the time in the world.

Just when I thought this rare musical performance couldn't get any better, the guy pounding on the pail swiftly jumped up on a streetlight. He started banging away at the top with his drumsticks. The sound is still etched in my mind. *Tink-tat-tink-tink-tat-tink-tink-tink.* Justin stared at the lonely pail on the sidewalk, and in the middle of playing, he jumped off the drum set and started playing on the pail.

His face lit up. He had never before played the pail, but he had no trouble following along and creating his own beats.

As the crowd cheered, a group of teenagers cleared a circle in the middle of the mob. They started breakdancing, spinning on their heads and doing flips. As Justin played the bucket, he couldn't stop staring at the dancers. He dropped the drumsticks on the sidewalk and made his way to the dancer's circle. He whipped off his sweater as he walked, and the crowd cried out, "Ooooh!" *Oh no you didn't!*

Justin busted out some moves that he had just learned from my friend Nathan. A natural performer, he egged on the young people that surrounded him by throwing his hands in the air, asking them if they wanted more. The crowd whooped and whistled.

After a few minutes, I could tell Justin was done. His attention span was running out. Sure enough, Justin looked at me and nodded his head. I knew it was time to go. By that time, there was so much activity going on between the drumming, the beats, and the dancing, it was easy for us to slip away almost unnoticed.

Justin's eyes were glowing. I could practically hear his heartbeat pounding wildly through his soaked T-shirt. "Mom, that was amazing!" he exclaimed, his face on fire from the adrenaline racing in his veins.

As we started walking away from the crowd, two older, raggedy-looking men started yelling at us, trying to grab our attention. Wearing mismatched layers of clothes covered with holes and sporting dirty, disheveled beards that hadn't seen a razor in what looked like months, the men appeared to be homeless. They yelled over the boisterous mob, "We gave the boy two dollars. It was all we had. He was great!" I was moved. I knew this was money they had earned panhandling.

One of them pointed to the guitar Justin had slung over his shoulder. "Can you play that?"

Justin and I nodded, still making our way through the crowd. I squeezed Justin's hand a little tighter and grabbed ahold of Nathan.

The two men continued to follow us as we walked. One of them shouted again, "Can we hear you play?" Justin nodded, and we motioned for them to follow us. If Nathan hadn't been with us, I wouldn't have entertained their request. It certainly wasn't something I made a habit of either.

The five of us walked farther down the block. As we neared the other end of the block, we could still hear the distant melodies of drums, pail, and lamppost. Justin got comfortable on the curb and carefully nestled the guitar on his lap. The two men beamed in delight, smelling like they hadn't showered in days. Justin wasn't fazed by their body odor or their dirty clothes. He was just happy he could make them smile.

The men crouched down on the empty street in front of Justin, anxious to hear a private concert. I heard Justin play the familiar chords of a song we sang in church. I was surprised that out of all the songs he could have chosen, from rock 'n' roll riffs to soulful tunes, Justin played that particular one. With a passion that was different from the way he'd played the drums and pail just minutes earlier, he started singing "Waves of Grace" from the depths of his heart.

> The walls are high, the walls are strong
> I've been locked in this castle
> That I've built for far too long
> You have surrounded me, a sea on every side
> The cracks are forming and I've got nowhere to hide
>
> Now I see
> The walls I've built are falling
> And Your waves of grace are washing over me

Lord, please reign in every part
I give my life to You, I open up my heart
I want to be like You, I want to seek Your face
O Lord, please wash me in Your awesome waves of grace

As my son sang, I watched the two hardened men, men who had seen enough of trouble to somehow end up on the streets. I didn't know their stories. I didn't know how they got here. I just knew that something about the song touched them in a deep place. I saw tears well up in the eyes of one man. He was embarrassed by his display of emotion and walked away, just far enough that we wouldn't see him cry. His buddy was also crying, though he didn't seem to mind if he had an audience. My heart bled for these two men. I was moved by their show of vulnerability in the moment.

When Justin strummed his last chord, he looked up, tears flooding his eyes. His voice cracked as he said, "Jesus loves you guys so much."

The men nodded. "We know, buddy, we know."

My son then ran a few feet down the block and bought the two men something to eat with his busking earnings. When he hugged them goodbye he said, "God bless you."

On the drive home, Justin cried. "Why can't we take them home, Mom? I don't want them to live outside," he begged, huge tears flooding down his cheeks.

I put my arm around my little boy, my heart aching from the compassion coming from his heart. I was proud of him—not just proud of his talent but proud of the character that was starting to take shape in his heart.

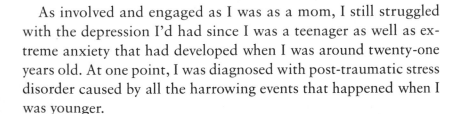

As involved and engaged as I was as a mom, I still struggled with the depression I'd had since I was a teenager as well as extreme anxiety that had developed when I was around twenty-one years old. At one point, I was diagnosed with post-traumatic stress disorder caused by all the harrowing events that happened when I was younger.

Particularly when Justin was around nine to about twelve years old, there were periods of time when I was so depressed that I had to force myself off the couch to play board games with him. Waking up was a chore in itself. Oh, what I would have given to sleep all day. I tried to pull myself up by the bootstraps and suck it up as best as I could. Some days were better than others.

I suffered from debilitating anxiety, which was so bad I would get physical pains in my chest and throat. I remember countless times when I would curl up in a fetal position and rock back and forth, crying out to God and begging him to take the anxiety away.

I tried a slew of different medications to find the most effective remedy, meds that wreaked havoc on my serotonin levels. Over a period of about twelve years, I probably tried close to sixty different medications to see what would be the best fit. None worked as I'd hoped.

Every time I filled a new prescription, I'd be hopeful for a cure. That this would be the med that would cure my anxiety. Relieve my depression. Make me into a better person, a new person who had more energy and less crippling anxiety. That it would remove that cloud that hung over my head. Though some meds helped for a while, none worked long term. There was no such thing as a magic pill for me.

In spite of how I felt, though, I knew where my priorities lay. I provided. I still showed up. I was there for Justin when he needed me. I cleaned. I cooked (okay, Kraft mac and cheese counts, right?). I took whatever little energy I had and poured it into caring for Justin. And I held on to my faith during this time, gaining strength and courage from God. In fact, I truly believe that some of my deepest moments of faith came from this time. But it wasn't easy.

Twelve

"Mom, there's a singing competition and I want to try out."

Twelve-year-old Justin had just come home from school and thrown his bulging backpack on the yellow shag carpet in the living room. How I hated that carpet. But for $140 a month in rent, what did I expect? Marble floors?

I immediately noticed Justin was still wearing his boots. A glistening trail of dirty melting snow ran from the front door to where he stood in the kitchen. *If I've told him once, I've told him a hundred times . . .*

"Helloooo." Justin annoyingly snapped his fingers in front of my face, trying to get my attention. "So what do you think? Can I try out or not?"

An audition? What on earth is he talking about? Is this about soccer? No, wait, didn't he mention something about singing? "Tell me about it," I said.

Justin hopped up on the chair next to me, fiddling with the papers that covered the table. A small goldfish would have had enough room to swim in the puddle of melted snow that had dripped off of his boots. "It's called Stratford Star. It's kinda like *American Idol*. Once you pass the auditions, you sing every week against other kids, and then judges vote you off and stuff until there's only three left."

Sounded like a competition for older kids. Justin wasn't even a teenager yet. "How old do you have to be?"

"Twelve to eighteen."

Wow. That was quite a range. I couldn't imagine a twelve-year-old competing with an eighteen-year-old. That's six years of more training, more experience, and more skill. I was actually surprised Justin even considered auditioning. Outside of busking on the streets of Stratford and Toronto purely for fun, he hadn't performed in front of an audience, certainly not onstage in front of people tasked with judging him. Not to mention that even though I knew he had a great voice and natural talent, he hadn't taken a single voice lesson in his life.

I had my reservations, but looking at Justin's eager face and seeing how he was dying for me to say yes, I decided to give him my blessing—just not before I offered words of caution. I didn't want to throw my son to the wolves or set him up for failure.

"Justin, listen to me. I believe in you and I know you can do anything. You're talented and smart. Whatever you choose to do, I know you'll be successful at it. I just want you to be aware of some realities." I walked Justin through a short tour of my involvement in the theatrical arts as a little girl. "I can't tell you how many times I auditioned for school plays and even community performances. I would pour my heart and soul into the auditions. And many times I believed wholeheartedly I'd get the part I wanted. But if I didn't, I was devastated. It broke my heart." Justin eagerly nodded, hopping off the chair to stand up.

"This is just an audition," I continued. "Whether or not you make it does not have any bearing on who you are or how talented you are."

Though Justin's eyes were locked with mine and I knew he was giving me his undivided attention, I was pretty sure he was rolling his eyes on the inside. *Yeah, yeah, yeah, Mom, I know. If I don't win, who cares? Yada yada yada.*

I wasn't going to say yes before I finished saying my piece. "And another thing. You have to remember, you're competing with people much older than you, as much as six years. That's a big difference, honey. I'm sure these contestants, especially the older ones, have been doing this for a while. It's probably not their first time. I'm sure they've had training and more experience and a ton of practice. You understand that, right?"

Justin stood there, impatiently anticipating my answer. "So that's a yes, Mom?"

I smiled. "Yes, Justin. You can try out."

"Yes!" he said, complete with a Tiger Woods fist pump.

But I still had just a little bit more to say. "And one more thing."

This time Justin groaned out loud.

"You're going to do your best, and you're gonna be awesome. And don't worry, if you don't get in, we'll get you some singing lessons, we'll practice a ton, and we'll get 'em next year!"

Justin took off to hang with his buddies. I made a phone call to find out more information and was told the auditions started on December 19, less than two weeks away.

⌒

Up to the day before his first audition, I prepared Justin the best I could. There's a fine line between encouraging your child and giving him or her a reality check. Sometimes the line is practically invisible. I had total faith in Justin. He obviously had talent oozing out of every pore in his body. I just wasn't sure he could hold his own against older kids who'd spent hundreds of hours practicing for this very moment.

We had barely two weeks before the auditions. We went into overdrive, asking my musician friends who loved and believed in Justin to help us however they could. Even though my son was a natural, he still had plenty to learn. Every day after school, Justin and I would drive over and practice in the youth center (not the Bunker), a drop-in place for teenagers in the community, which had opened its doors for any wannabe contestant who wanted to use their sound equipment and karaoke machine.

Justin wasn't the only one preparing for the auditions. Practically everyone who planned on auditioning took advantage. By four o'clock in the afternoon, the place was packed with teens playing Ping-Pong and foosball, shooting hoops on the half-court with their squeaky sneakers, and practicing for the upcoming auditions. It was a madhouse.

My musician friends came with us a few times to teach Justin about the basics of performing—things like how to hold a microphone, how to develop stage presence, and how to sing and groove with the music so it looks natural, not forced or awkward. While Justin had to learn about the basics, he didn't have to learn the "it" factor. I knew it. My friends knew it. People at the youth center who watched him practice knew it. Whatever "it" was, Justin had it.

When the kids who were practicing for the competition took their turns at the mic to rehearse, they battled against the chaotic soundtrack of noisy and obnoxious teenage chatter and bouncing balls. One of the youth workers noted that when it was Justin's turn to practice, the room fell silent. Everyone stopped what they were doing. She commented how all eyes turned toward Justin.

My son practiced all the time, everywhere—in the car, in the shower, at his grandparents' house. Sometimes he even practiced on the hockey bench when he was waiting to get thrown into a game or before he'd run some drills. Justin wasn't even aware he was singing out loud most times. Once he was on the bench and his buddy whipped off his helmet. "Dude, you realize you're singing, right?"

My son and I bonded during this time. Without an athletic bone in my body, I admit I had a tough time relating to his love for sports. But when it came to music and the arts, we definitely found common ground.

As Justin prepared for his audition, I was more nervous than he was. But he (and nine other competitors) impressed the judges enough to make it through the auditions. There would be three weekly performance days, on which the contestants would sing two or three songs a night, until the final three were chosen. Those remaining competitors would then sing for the final time on January 27, 2007.

Justin and I kicked it into high gear. Together we picked songs that showcased his unique sound—my son definitely had some soul in him—and that he enjoyed singing. The latter was the most important requirement. The songs we picked ran the gamut of styles and feelings—from the lullaby-like melody of "Angel" by Sarah McLachlan to the catchy pop groove of "3 AM" by Matchbox Twenty to the universal favorite "Respect" by Aretha Franklin to his first taste at rapping with Lil' Bow Wow's "Basketball." We had a bit of everything, from pop to country to R&B.

When Justin took the stage for his rendition of "Angel" and I aimed the video camera in his direction, I was nervous, probably more than he was. I quickly scoped out the audience filled with kids and parents, contestants and supporters. I wasn't the only anxious one in the room. The nervous energy was almost tangible. Some girls couldn't stop talking or fidgeting and had to be shushed by their moms or annoyed parents around them. Some kids were visibly nervous and leaned into their parents, who protectively wrapped an arm around their shoulders. Then there were the serious contestants, the ones who appeared confident and calm, quietly staking out their competition.

When Justin grabbed hold of the mic at the sound of the first notes of "Angel," he looked a little uncomfortable, at least not as comfortable as he would look a few performances later. And his outfit? Oh my goodness. Looking back, what were we thinking? We never thought to choose an outfit to complement his song of choice. There he was, singing this beautifully hypnotic melody wearing a huge sweatshirt, a baseball cap, and a pair of oversized sneakers, hip-hop style. One of the judges actually mentioned his outfit. "Pay attention to what you're wearing," he suggested. "Your wardrobe reflects your song."

Once Justin started singing, however, his outfit was the furthest thing from anyone's mind. He sounded amazing. His powerful voice echoed throughout the auditorium that was so quiet you could hear a pin drop. As my little boy sang the soothing tune, my heart melted. I could barely hold up the video camera. Do you know how hard it is to record when tears are welling up in your eyes? I videotaped every performance. I hated watching Justin through the lens and the videos are proof. They're dark, shaky, and blurry. But hey, I got the footage.

Justin blew me away on this song, as he would every song he sang. I knew if the judges didn't move him through that round, I would be just as proud. I stared at my twelve-year-old son onstage as he ended his performance with the sound of applause ringing in his ears. His smile was as big as the auditorium. It was obvious—he belonged onstage. It was home.

The truth is, Justin surprised me. He was the only twelve-year-old, the youngest competitor in the entire competition. So when he made it through, I was ecstatic. My jock of a son, who had never had a singing lesson, who had a late start preparing for the contest, who didn't even know how to properly hold a microphone two weeks earlier, made it past the first round. I'll never forget when it was the first judge's turn to critique Justin's performance. She was so over-come with emotion and tears, she had to wait a turn so she could compose herself and ultimately applaud his efforts.

The more Justin performed, the more his confidence grew. Each song was a little better. His body loosened up more. His personality started coming through. His presence got stronger. Even his outfits got better. And the audience started to fall in love with this adorable adolescent boy with the charming and contagious grin.

While some of the other contestants who remained in the com-petition week after week were better trained, had more experience, and were more polished, Justin had a certain je ne sais quoi. He had a raw talent that made his mistakes forgivable and sometimes even unnoticeable. The crowd certainly didn't seem to mind how young and inexperienced Justin was. They were just blown away by his natural confidence on stage.

The judges gushed after his performances, aside from the one constructive criticism to choose an appropriate wardrobe. They called him a "natural born performer" and "Mr. Personality" and told him to "never lose that soul passion."

And then there were the girls. There were always the girls. Not long after Justin's first audition, word started spreading like wildfire across town about this cute kid who could sing. I remember walking into the auditorium one week and noticing more commotion than usual at the entrance. The closer we got, the louder the screams. With ponytails whipping in the wind like lassoes, a pack of preteen girls jumped up and down, invisible springs strapped to their feet.

As Justin passed, they squealed. Some of them seemed almost embarrassed at their bold enthusiasm, but when Justin smiled and waved and thanked them for coming, they screamed louder. There were only a handful of them, but I tell you what, they were loud. Even today, I am amazed at the sheer volume a tiny group of girls can make; three of them can easily sound like ten.

By the final week, the audience had grown so much that only a few empty seats remained in the place. There were more girls. More screaming girls. The screaming girls started bringing homemade signs that read in bright glittery letters "I love you, Justin Bieber" and "I vote for Justin." What a taste of things to come. After one of his performances, one judge, amused by my son's fans, joked, "I've been playing for twenty-five years and I've never had girls coming up to me like this."

Before Justin took the stage and after he performed during the final round, the crowd would chant his name. Girls, mostly. Twenty or thirty of them. "Justin! Justin! Justin!" The rhythmic chant was hypnotic. The chanting alternated with the screaming, voices so loud the judges had to plug their ears. Outside of the proud mama feeling, I found the whole spectacle hilarious. But there wasn't a doubt in my mind—Justin was the crowd favorite. (I know, I'm a little biased.)

My mom and Bruce faithfully showed up to each of Justin's performances, as did Jeremy and our extended families (grandparents, aunts, uncles, cousins—you name it, they were there). Unfortunately, Justin's grandmother Kate, Jeremy's mom, lived a five-hour plane ride away and wasn't able to come. She loved her grandson, and not being able to support him in person devastated her. Justin and I knew she felt left out. He adored Kate and wanted to somehow make her feel involved.

We were at the house one day, Justin preparing for the next day's competition. He was belting out one of the songs he was thinking of using when he stopped cold. The melody turned into a yell.

"Mom!"

I was washing the dishes, my arms covered in suds and the rush of running water drowning out sounds except for the clanging of dirty dishes. I was about to yell back, "What?" but Justin was too impatient.

"Mom!"

This time Justin barreled into the kitchen like a horse that broke out of the gate. I was so startled I almost dropped a drinking glass on the linoleum floor.

I turned toward him, the dishwater dripping on my jeans. "What's up, honey?"

"Can we put the videos of the competition on YouTube for Grandma Kate?"

And that's the inception of Justin's YouTube journey. He went online not for the random local. Not for the stranger in the next town. Not for the province of Ontario. Not for the world. Justin posted the videos for his grandmother.

Because I was familiar with technology, I was able to not only upload the videos but also tag them for the search engine in such a way that his grandmother and even other relatives and family friends could easily find them in the YouTube video jungle. I even set up a channel specifically for Justin's videos called "Kidrauhl." The name was spun from his dad's online screen name, "Lordrauhl."

Grandma Kate loved the fact she could watch Justin online. It made her feel special. She was so proud of her grandson, she left one of the very first comments: "Well done, Justin. Hope the other one will be posted too, with the standing O intact!" Ironically, his first comment was from a stranger: "Holy [blank] . . . this kid is awesome." His cousin followed up with, "Yep, he's awesome. He will be famous. He's only 12 now . . ."

Justin made it to the final three with "Basketball" by Lil' Bow Wow and "So Sick" by Ne-Yo. He gave it his all during these performances. As the opening beats sounded on "Basketball," Justin strutted onstage, raising his hands and clapping. He didn't have to psych up the crowd to join in; almost everyone in the audience instantly clapped along with the beat, some even cheering him on.

I couldn't help but think back on Justin's first performances. He hadn't quite connected with the audience, and they hadn't warmed up to him. It was a struggle for Justin to get them moving. He tried getting them excited and encouraged them to clap as he sang, but it was no use. Outside of the few people who kept the beat, the auditorium was deathly quiet.

His final performances were nothing like that. As the crowd roared during the introduction of "Basketball," Justin broke out in a breakdance windmill, then a stall. The cheering was so loud you couldn't even hear the music. He grabbed the mic to start rapping and threw out his baseball cap into the audience. Girls screamed. Parents laughed. The judges couldn't help but smile and shake their heads. This was it. The audience had a spot in their heart reserved for Justin. He knew how to entertain them. He knew how to get them hyped. And he definitely knew how to make the girls squeal.

He was on fire as he flew through the song, egged on by the boisterous crowd. On this song and his last of the evening, Justin did what he did best. He gave the audience what they wanted—an awesome performance. His passion was evident. It streamed out of him and melted into a puddle at the feet of the crowd. You can't teach passion like that. You can't manufacture that kind of spirit. And you can't fake it. You either have it or you don't.

Justin was in the final round with seasoned female performers. When he performed "Respect" and busted out moves during the sax solo, the crowd went bananas. Wearing his signature baseball cap backward and baggy pants, he let loose a playful rendition of air sax and didn't even miss a beat when the microphone fell out of his hand. The audience laughed and Justin broke out in a teasing smirk. He picked up the mic and continued his passionate air sax solo. The snafu made Justin even more lovable, especially because it didn't affect his performance in the least.

When the winners were to be announced at the end of the performances, Justin stood onstage with the two girls. Being so young, he looked tiny, like a grasshopper in the land of giants. I knew if he didn't win, I'd be somewhat bummed, but the fact that he shared the stage with talented singers who'd had years of vocal lessons and coaching was an honor in itself. I was proud of him. Proud that he took a chance to even audition and proud that he made it to the top three. Justin's cheering section of girls was screaming so loudly in support I was sure their voices would be gone by the end of the night. Family and friends joined the hysteria, keeping our fingers crossed and anxiously hoping that he would come in first place.

I know Justin was disappointed when sixteen-year-old Kristen Hawley was announced as the winner. But he knew not to be a sore loser. Whether he was playing hockey or soccer, I always taught him how to be a good sport. As the crowd cheered for Kristen and her face glowed, soaking in the win, Justin reached his hand out to hers. He firmly shook it and whispered, "Congratulations." That small gesture touched my heart. As confident and bold as he was as a competitor, he always gave respect where it was due. I admired that about my son. And it made me even more proud.

I could see the disappointment building as we chitchatted afterward with the crowd. Judges, friends, family, and random members of the community came up to us, shaking Justin's hand and telling him how awesome he did, even if he didn't come home with first place. My son was polite, nodding and saying "Thank you," shrugging and smiling when others told him he could always try again next year.

I knew he was putting on a brave front. He couldn't hide from his mother how devastated he was. All mamas can tell what's really going on behind a mask. Justin was born with a fierce competitive streak. He loved to win—at everything—so losing crushed him. He had poured his heart and soul into the competition. And week after week Justin beat the odds. Week after week, the crowd fell more in love with him. Nursing a loss was like losing a battle. As one of the judges patted his back and praised his performances, I knew it was only a matter of time before those raw emotions of disappointment would surface.

We drove home in silence. From the corner of my eye I could see the tears welling up. I knew that no matter how many times I told him I was proud of him, no matter how many times I told him he had done an amazing job, my reassurances wouldn't even put a dent in how devastated he felt.

Justin was always hardest on himself. He's still that way today. If at the end of a concert, he doesn't feel like the performance was up to his exceptionally high standards—even though everyone else thought he did an outstanding job—he's miserable. Justin has always been a perfectionist and works hard to be the best, whether he's playing soccer or hockey or performing onstage in front of thousands of people.

What started as a way to connect with his grandmother morphed into random strangers finding the videos and even making specific requests. Justin and I started recording oodles of videos of him singing all kinds of songs. But we didn't just make videos for YouTube. I have thousands of videos of Justin simply being silly. He would fool around and make crazy faces and sounds, beatbox, and even make up raps.

I got a kick out of every performance he did—whether it was a song for his YouTube fans or him breakdancing to Michael Jackson in front of no one else but me. When Justin sang or played music, I couldn't help but notice how much soul and passion he emanated. When I watch these old home videos, absent of professional lighting, proper audio and visual equipment, or even a good videographer (my skills still have not improved), I love how raw and organic they look and sound. They are the most natural expressions of my son's talent. Where he began. How it all started.

I stayed awake many nights past midnight, a Tim Hortons caffeine fix to my right and my laptop opened in front of me. While Justin slept, I was up monitoring the YouTube channel, uploading new videos, keeping track of stats, and checking comments to make sure they weren't offensive. Maintaining the channel was time consuming and required a lot of energy and effort, but I loved it. I looked forward to it. It was something fun to do. Every time I posted a video, I would refresh the page every two seconds to see the new comments and the change in view count.

Friends and family weren't the only ones watching Justin's videos. I had strategically tagged all his videos by the song title and artist, so searches for that particular song or artist would bring up Justin's video. That's how so many people were able to find his videos so effortlessly. While comments came in pretty quickly after we posted the first video, they started pouring in over the next few weeks from people all over the world.

"Wow, dude. You're pretty good."

"Nice voice, you're so talented."

"Justin, you're amazing. Watching this makes me want to marry you, lol."

"He's going to change the world."

YouTube is different today than it was back when we were first posting Justin's videos online. Back then, YouTube had thirty or forty different awards in different categories—ranging from "Most viewed of the day" to "Most favorited" and "Most responded to," to name a few. The site would give out a number of different awards every day. One afternoon while Justin was gearing up for a hockey game, I noticed one of his videos got a YouTube award. It was his first, something like "10th most viewed video of the day."

I was so excited I started laughing. Right before my eyes my little boy, who really wasn't so little anymore, was attracting a crazy amount of attention on the internet. "Justin, you're not gonna believe this," I called out while he grabbed a Gatorade out of the fridge and started chugging. "You got a YouTube award."

Justin looked at me and nodded. "Cool," he said with a smile. My son was nowhere near as excited as I was about his videos and online following. His channel was on my radar all the time, even at work.

Freelance jobs designing websites were slow in coming, so I took a part-time job at Conestoga College doing administrative work. I was also still teaching some basic computer courses to senior citizens at nearby nursing homes and giving private home lessons. Whenever I had a break in the middle of showing sweet old ladies how to use social media to stay connected with their grandkids, I would check the YouTube channel. How many more comments did Justin get? What did they think of his new song? How many people viewed his video since last night?

When Justin would get home from school, I was a nonstop blabberfest, giving him a play-by-play update on the responses from his videos. I was a vocal Energizer Bunny. My chatter eventually got on his nerves. Even proud mamas need to back off sometimes and give their child a little space. I admit, it was hard for me to simmer down my enthusiasm, despite Justin groaning at my incessant status reports of his growing fan base.

After his channel started gaining popularity, I cocreated a YouTube channel with a man named James, a statistics genius and video editor, whom I met in an online community. We designed the channel so well-known YouTube kids could collaborate on videos together. Through working together, we formed a friendship, and he ended up helping me with Justin's YouTube channel. It was great to have someone to share my excitement with since Justin seemed so nonchalant about his rising online fame.

The success of his home music videos snowballed in the blink of an eye. Six months after Justin lost the Stratford Star competition, his YouTube popularity was at such a peak, monitoring his channel was like having a part-time job. I was diligent at first in sifting out the negative comments from haters—and boy, some people who had never met Justin and didn't know anything about him had some awful things to say; I don't know how people can be that mean to anybody, let alone a child. But the comments poured in faster and in such great numbers (as many as a few hundred a day) that they became impossible to monitor.

I would have needed to dedicate every single hour of my day to keep track of everything. For a short while, James helped me pick up the slack (thanks, James!) until finally we had a team of our own to help manage the channel. Ironically, when Justin's manager Scooter came on board, he and I would obsessively monitor every video of Justin's, just like James and I used to do, except on a larger scale.

Soon enough, Justin was a YouTube celebrity. That was enough for me. It was such a fun, entertaining, and exhilarating experience, I couldn't even imagine what real stardom was like. Frankly, I didn't even want to imagine that kind of life.

His popularity got to the point where it wasn't just random strangers who had something to say about his rising YouTube fame. He piqued the interest of a few nationally syndicated talk shows that wanted him on their program. As honored as I felt, I was nowhere near ready to even consider those opportunities.

Thirteen

I couldn't believe the number of emails Justin started getting through the YouTube channel from managers and various record label executives who wanted to pilot his career and turn him into a star. It was all very overwhelming. And strange. I was used to having an inbox full of messages from fans commenting how cute Justin was and how much they loved him. As it was, I couldn't keep up with those comments and messages.

So I didn't. But not just because I didn't have the time. I didn't want my son anywhere near that path. I figured all the people who were hounding us were determined only to turn him into a cash cow to fill their pockets. Isn't that how the music business works? So thanks but no thanks. We're not interested.

I ignored the emails, having no intention of showing them to Justin. The truth was, I had a pipe dream that Justin was going to become a worship leader or youth pastor. All my talented musician friends were worship leaders, so I assumed that Justin's talent would warrant him treading down that same path. When the emails about music opportunities kept on coming, it challenged me to look outside my bubble.

I was also hesitant because I was afraid. Everyone knows what happens to many child artists. I had heard all the horror stories about the music industry as a whole. I didn't want to be naïve in thinking Justin would be immune from the dangers and temptations in that business. Almost a teenager, he would have plenty to deal with in high school on his own. So according to my initial calculations, there was no way God was opening the door for Justin to enter the music world.

As a praying mother, I did just that—I prayed about the opportunities. Because of my fear and my then-limited perception of the way God operates, I unintentionally prayed from a place of doubt. "Surely this isn't Your will, right?" I guess in a way I acted as if I knew better than God. I could better protect my son. I could better determine his future. "And if this is Your will," I said to God, "You mean You're opening the door for him to sing in the Christian music industry, right?"

Immediately I was reminded of a verse in the Bible: "You are light for the world. A city cannot be hidden when it is located on a hill. No one lights a lamp and puts it under a basket. Instead, everyone who lights a lamp puts it on a lamp stand. Then its light shines on everyone in the house. In the same way let your light shine in front of people" (Matt. 5:14–16).

I heard God speak into my heart. *How is Justin supposed to be a light in the world if he's not in the world?*

"But he's only thirteen," I argued out loud. "He's not grounded. I know You have a hook in his heart, but he doesn't have any roots. This doesn't feel safe."

Do you trust me?

Sigh.

Apparently, not enough. The answer was obvious.

When Justin was a baby, I dedicated his life to God in a special ceremony at my church, much the same way that Hannah dedicated

Samuel in the Bible (see 1 Sam. 1). I remember praying that day, asking God to raise Justin up to be a leader and a voice to his generation.

This story came to mind as I was praying about Justin's future one evening. I felt God telling me to trust Him. To let go of my plans for Justin. It was time for me to give up creating the kind of future for my son that I wanted him to have, that I thought he should have. And that's when I finally started paying attention to the emails and calls coming in. I even considered the possibility that God could be the one opening those very doors.

In the middle of 2007, a manager from Atlanta named Scooter tried to contact me through several avenues. He was relentless. He sent emails to me through the YouTube channel. He tried to get through to other people who he hoped would get in contact with me for him. This guy messaged one of my top friends on MySpace, called Justin's great-aunt whom my son had never met (in addition to anyone with the last name Bieber where we lived), and tried to get in touch with me via the Avon Theatre, the venue in the YouTube video where he had watched Justin sing. All these people called me and left message after message that some young guy named Scooter with a Gmail address was trying to reach me about Justin.

Probably one of Scooter's boldest moves was when he called Justin's school by way of the Stratford Board of Education. It wasn't common knowledge that Justin had a YouTube identity. He was a jock, a cool and popular kid. Most of the students didn't know how he spent his extra time outside of sports. Justin kept his entertaining hobbies on the down low. Although his classmates knew he'd competed in the Stratford Star, no one knew Justin continued singing.

When Scooter's messages finally reached the school, someone on staff started streaming his videos on the TV monitors in the hallway the next day. When Justin walked into school that morning, a gigantic screen blasted one of his YouTube videos. Now everyone knew. Though he was embarrassed by the attention because he had a reputation as a jock, not a singer, there was one advantage—the girls. They were excited for him, proud of their local up-and-coming YouTube sensation. And they weren't shy about letting Justin know.

After Scooter unintentionally outed Justin, he continued to track me down, and I continued to keep my distance. I didn't know much about him other than what I was told from the people in my life he was contacting. I knew his name was Scooter Braun. He had name-dropped popular music stars, so I knew he'd worked with famous artists like Usher, Justin Timberlake, and Britney Spears. I also knew he had a Gmail address. The latter two bits of information kept me from calling him back.

I wasn't impressed by name-dropping. I'd heard it all before from other managers and so-called record execs who promised they had worked with or were friends with that pop star or this celebrity. It was usually a long stretch from the truth. Scooter's Gmail address also made me suspicious. Why wouldn't he have an email address with his record label name? All the other emails I got came from reputable management groups, like joeschmoe@so-and-so-company.

I admired his persistence, but I thought he was more of a joke than a realistic option. I finally called him just to get him to stop calling everyone I knew. I used a computer line so I could block my name and number. No need to give him a direct channel to reach me.

I'd had a long day. I had just completed a massive project at the college, and I had taught Microsoft Word classes that afternoon. I was exhausted. My feet hurt from standing for hours, and all I had eaten the entire day was a stale bagel. I only planned for a five-minute conversation with Scooter. I didn't have much to say other than "Please stop calling." I had more important things to do. I wanted to spend the rest of the evening indulging in a long, hot bubble bath.

I dialed Scooter's number, but my mind was on my much-needed R and R.

"This is Scooter."

"Hi," I said in a flat tone of voice. "This is Pattie Mallette, Justin Bieber's mom."

"Ms. Mallette, thank you so much for calling me back!" Scooter couldn't hide his excitement if he tried.

I started right into my planned "thanks but no thanks" speech, looking at my watch to see what time it was. Before I knew it, my rehearsed speech turned into a long-winded, two-hour phone conversation. We chatted away like long-lost friends.

Scooter told me how he found Justin on YouTube and how my son's talent blew him away. Then he told me about himself, what exactly he did for a living. "Just google me," he suggested. "You can find out information about some of the projects I've done and people I've worked with." (Later that night, I did search for him. I laugh about it now, but the first thing that popped up was a magazine article titled "Scooter Braun Is the Hustla." To the right of that title was a picture of Scooter on a cell phone flanked by two hot blondes pawing him. It wasn't the most encouraging first impression for a mother of a thirteen-year-old boy.)

While Scooter was definitely a fast and smooth talker—hey, it's what he does for a living—something about him seemed genuine and warm. The conversation took off in all sorts of interesting directions. Scooter and I talked about everything from Justin and his potential career in the music industry to our faith. He mentioned looking at my MySpace page and seeing I was a Christian.

"I'm Jewish," he told me. "Is that going to be a problem?"

How silly, I thought. "Of course not," I answered. "Jesus was Jewish." Sure, my initial thought pattern in this process had been a bit shortsighted. I had first approached these opportunities thinking Justin was going to be in the Christian music circle or at least would be represented by a Christian manager. But I had nothing personal against anyone of any faith, and I would never discriminate against someone's talent, intelligence, or skills just because they didn't share my beliefs.

Faith was important to me, and I had raised Justin with those beliefs and values. So of course I had hoped Justin would work with a manager who could continue to instill those same faith principles in his life. But the way this journey was unfolding, it didn't matter what plans or wants I had for Justin's future; it was obvious God had other ones.

Scooter ended the conversation by inviting us to meet him in Atlanta. "I'll introduce you to some people down here so you can see
for yourself that I'm legit, that I'm not blowing smoke. You don't
have to sign anything. You don't have to promise to do anything. No
pressure. No obligations. If you come and you hate it, consider this
a free paid vacation to Atlanta. At least think about it."

As persistent as Scooter was, I have to say he was never a jerk and
never tried to bully his way into Justin's life. I was always honest
about any fears or reservations I had, and Scooter delicately handled
our relationship with the perfect balance of tenacity and patience.
He understood my suspicions about the music industry and always
made me feel there was no pressure. So sure, of course I could think
about meeting him.

I took time to pray after that phone call. There was no reason to
talk to Justin about anything yet; I still had to mull things over in
my head. It would have been easy for me to decide what was best for
us based on what I wanted in a manager, but ultimately I wanted to
hear what God's best was. His ways were obviously very different
from my ways.

At the time Jeremy lived in Winnipeg, twelve hundred miles away
from Stratford. Though he and Justin didn't see each other regularly,
simply because of the distance, Jeremy and I had conversations during this time. He was both happy and worried sick about the potential
opportunity. We shared the same cautiousness.

After Scooter's offer, I talked to my spiritual parents John and
Sue Brown and Ivan and Isabel, as well as other spiritual leaders at
my church whom I trusted. When I met with these different people,
I told them about my conversation with Scooter and Justin's potential opportunity in the music business. I also regurgitated my
fears about why I didn't think it was a good idea. I strongly pled
my case. "It's dangerous," I said. "It's not safe. Justin is only thirteen years old. He's a boy who still has a ton of growing up to do."
Despite my best efforts to convince these mentors why it was best
for us to ignore these open doors, every one of them felt a peace
about it.

Everyone except me. While I appreciated their sentiment, it still wasn't enough for me. That's when I remembered Gideon.

⁓

The Bible tells a story in Judges 6 about a man named Gideon. He wasn't necessarily the most confident or secure man around. Nor was he winning any awards for courage or bravery. But for some reason God chose him to be a warrior and do some pretty important things for the nation of Israel. Unsure of himself and unsure whether God was really leading him, Gideon prayed one night for confirmation. He laid a wool fleece on the ground and said, "Lord, if I wake up in the morning and the fleece is wet with dew but the ground dry, I'll know these plans are really from You."

Gideon woke up to dry ground and a wet fleece. But he still wasn't convinced. That night, he asked God for another sign, the reverse. And the next morning, Gideon found his fleece was dry and the ground wet with dew. He got his confirmation.

Like Gideon, I had fleeces of my own. I asked God for two things: confirmation that Scooter was supposed to be Justin's manager (my pastor's peace wasn't confirmation enough) and an entertainment attorney. The latter may have seemed premature, but I didn't want to even consider meeting with Scooter unless we had legitimate representation. I also didn't want an attorney who was just a little bit familiar with the entertainment industry. I had been warned by a friend who had been burned; she strongly urged me to get a good lawyer. I wanted a big shot, someone who represented major players.

Justin's talent and the massive amount of attention he was getting from his YouTube fame motivated me to make sure we were prepared, that we weren't walking into a minefield wearing a blindfold. I didn't want to find myself getting cornered or locked into a contract or deal, despite Scooter's assurances there were no strings attached to our meeting. The fact was, I didn't know a thing about contracts, negotiations, or anything relating to the music business. I knew absolutely nothing.

It seemed like an impossible fleece, at least in my eyes. I barely had enough money to put food on the table. I'd heard top-notch entertainment attorneys cost up to $900 an hour. Nine hundred dollars an hour? Are you kidding me? That year I barely pulled in $10,000 between all the jobs I worked. I couldn't come up with $900 in a month! I would have to either win the lottery, get an impossibly high raise, or find an attorney who would work with us for free.

It wasn't long before one of my prayers was answered. Scooter called one day to see if I had been thinking about his offer and how I felt about moving forward.

I was up front with him. "I can't even think of making a commitment until I have an entertainment lawyer. I'll be honest. This whole thing sounds exciting and glamorous, an amazing opportunity. But I'm not making any decisions or even entertaining the offer without a lawyer, and frankly, I can't afford one, so I'm not sure how far this can go."

Scooter didn't hesitate a half a second. "Oh, that's easy, Pattie. I'll make some calls. I know a couple lawyers who work on a percentage rate. They don't require any upfront costs. I know how talented Justin is, and I'm confident once they see his talent, plenty of attorneys will want to represent him."

A few days later, I got a phone call from one of the top entertainment lawyers in the business, who agreed to take Justin on as a client. He told me that he'd worked with Scooter for a long time and had a lot of faith in him. "If Scooter thinks your son has potential," he told me, "he's probably right." This lawyer had also watched Justin's YouTube videos and could see for himself how talented Justin was. After we got off the phone, I did some research and found out that he represented a lot of big names in the industry. He was legit, exactly what I had in mind.

I was shocked. There it was, my fleece, right before my eyes. When I had thought of the idea of possibly having a top entertainment lawyer to give us advice, it sounded preposterous. Impossible. Against all odds. I never imagined it would realistically pan out. But somehow, and without much effort on my part, I found myself with a well-versed, experienced, and sharp attorney who knew the entertainment world inside and out.

One fleece down, one to go.

I still had to talk to Justin before confirming the trip to meet with Scooter. Surprisingly, it was one of the easiest conversations I've ever had with my son, considering the topic was such a big deal, so life changing.

I had just come home from work, ready to get out of my business casual clothes and into a pair of sweats. I sank into my favorite spot on the living room couch and opened Justin's YouTube page.

A hundred more comments on that one video. Wow!

Hmm, someone wants Justin to do something by Michael Jackson. Ugh! How could that guy say that about Justin? He's just a kid.

Oh my gosh! We got another award for "Most responded to" video.

As I started eyeballing the new emails that had come in the last few hours, I heard the key jiggle in the front door. "Hey, Mom, what's up?" Justin barreled through the apartment and made his way over to me wearing a backward baseball cap and a hoodie. He looked like he was coming home only to go right back out. He was always busy doing something—playing sports, going to the skate park, playing video games at his friend's house. If he wasn't singing and I wasn't holding a video camera, it was like pulling teeth to get him to sit with me and talk. He was the same two-year-old boy with wild energy, a toddler always on the move.

"Sit with me for a minute, Justin. I want to talk to you about something."

Justin plunked down on the couch, leaning in to give me a kiss on the cheek.

I took a deep breath, fully intending to keep the conversation light and casual. I didn't want Justin to feel I was pressuring him in the slightest. "Do you like singing?"

"Um, yeah."

"Do you love singing?"

"Sure."

"What do you want to be when you grow up, Justin?"

"A professional hockey or soccer player, probably. I don't know. Why?" He started fiddling with his shoelaces.

"All right. Now, if you had the opportunity to sing and play music as a career, would you do it? Or even think about it?"

Justin sighed, annoyed at the litany of questions. I wonder if he had an inkling where I was going with this. "Yeah, probably. Why are you asking me all these questions?"

I looked at my just-barely-a-teenager boy. I doubted he understood the magnitude of what I would be asking him. I doubted he understood some of the sacrifices it would require. I doubted he understood that this wasn't a joke, something we could afford to take lightly, like picking a new hobby or deciding which pair of soccer cleats to buy.

"Well, we have the opportunity to go to Atlanta to meet with some people and check it out. What do you think about that? You want to give it a shot?"

I closed my eyes, almost hoping he wouldn't be interested so we could wrap up this talk and call it a day. We could go back to our normal lives without me needing to wrestle with these unique decisions about his future. I could continue living in my comfort zone. If Justin had said no, I would have called Scooter that very second and pulled the plug on that and future offers. And I would have kept making and posting videos of Justin only for as long as he wanted.

But Justin didn't say no. His eyes lit up. He said, "Yeah, sure! When do we get to go?"

I set up a Skype call with Scooter. I wasn't going to make the two-hour flight without Justin first meeting Scooter. The two of them hit it off immediately. Scooter's young at heart, fun, and great with kids, and Justin quickly took to him. It was settled. Though I wasn't going to make any decisions about Scooter until I got confirmation, we were going to Atlanta.

All systems were go, but I still wondered about my second fleece, my prayer to know without a doubt that Scooter was meant to be Justin's manager. From the outside, he seemed like a pretty good guy. He sounded like he knew what he was doing. But still, I needed clear confirmation, not just peace.

A few days before our trip, I was running an errand downtown. I wanted to pick up some chocolate at Rhéo Thompson Candies, our world-famous local chocolate shop. I parked my car by a cute café and walked a few extra blocks, grateful for the sunny day and fresh air.

"Hey, Pattie," I heard someone call out. I turned around and saw my friend Nathan, the same guy who organized a fundraiser for Justin for a drum set. He was walking with a young man I didn't know. The guy he was with was looking at me weird. Not in a creepy way, though. It almost seemed like he wanted to say something but kept choking back the words. Finally he said, "I'm not sure how this is going to sound or if you're going to think this is crazy, but I really believe I have a word from God for you."

My heart started pounding. "Sure, let me have it," I answered.

"I feel like you have been thinking or praying about working with a Jewish man. And I feel like God is saying 'yes, yes, and yes.' The favor of God is on him. God blesses everything this man touches."

I was in awe. It couldn't have been any clearer. This was someone I had never met telling me the answer to my prayer.

"Wow! Thanks! You are right on. I've been praying about this very thing." I marveled at how God can operate in the strangest of places, in the strangest of ways, and through the lives of perfect strangers. We spoke for a few minutes, and I shared with them about the potential opportunity that was awaiting Justin and how reluctant I had been to pursue it.

God had answered my second fleece. It was official. I knew that at least for this season, Scooter was the right choice. I knew he would be the one who would play a significant role in Justin's life and music career. I was expectant but somewhat nervous. I hadn't a clue what lay ahead. I hadn't a clue what doors our trip to Atlanta would open. Frankly, I would never have even imagined the possibilities in my wildest dreams.

CHAPTER

Fourteen

Justin and I boarded the plane for our two-hour-plus flight to Atlanta. Right before we stepped into the aisle to make our way to our seats, a pretty flight attendant tapped Justin on the shoulder. "Would you like a tour of the cockpit?" she asked, winking discreetly at me. "We're not allowed to do this, but the captain said you can come and check it out." Only moments earlier, I had mentioned to one of the crew that it was Justin's first time on a plane.

As the rest of the passengers squeezed past us, many of them with carry-on bags that looked way too big for the overhead bins, Justin exploded in a mile-wide smile. "Sure!" I thought it was unusual, in light of the security aftermath of 9/11, that the crew allowed Justin in the cockpit, but we definitely appreciated the gesture.

Surrounded by an endless array of buttons, lights, and switches, the captain and co-pilot gave a brief overview of the flight systems. Spellbound by the flashing lights, Justin didn't say much except "Cool" and "No way!" I rummaged through my purse to find a camera, the one I'd have glued to my hand the entire trip, and snapped a photo of Justin. My son grinned with one hand clutching the airplane throttle. His long, dirty-blonde hair peeked through the oversized hat the pilot was kind enough to let him wear. I had a feeling being able to tour the cockpit was the beginning of many firsts for Justin on this trip.

As the roar of the engines sounded when the plane started down the runway, Justin pressed his face against the window. We started picking up speed, the jet rumbling louder. The nose of the airplane began to lift, gently pushing us back into our seats. Justin was thunderstruck. "We're going! We're going! We're going! We're almost there!" The plane continued to rise, the last touch of the wheels grazing the runway. Hit with a sinking feeling in his belly as we soared into the open blue sky, Justin moaned, "Oh, my stomach. My stomach is like, bleahh!" But he quickly recovered, staring out the window as the city below became smaller and smaller. "This is awesome," Justin burst out. "I can see everything!"

When we touched down in Atlanta and made our way through the busiest airport in the United States, we were nervously excited. Justin darted his eyes every which way, scoping out anything interesting or unusual. He had the same curious and inquisitive look as when we roamed the streets of downtown Toronto when he was six. But he wasn't a little kid anymore; he was a teenager. Too old to hold my hand as we battled the midday crowd in the terminal, but still young enough that he needed me (though as a typical teenager, he probably wouldn't admit it).

I sighed. *He's growing up too fast.*

"C'mon, Mom, let's go!" Justin snapped me out of my musings.

"I'm coming, I'm coming," I muttered, playfully annoyed.

We made it through to the baggage claim area, calling Scooter as we walked to tell him we had arrived.

"Awesome! Look for the purple Mercedes out front," he told us. "You can't miss it."

We saw Scooter as soon as we exited the terminal. He broke out in a winning smile when he hopped out of his car to grab our bags. He gave me a warm hug and high-fived Justin. "It's so good to see you guys. How was your flight?"

As we sped off toward downtown Atlanta, whizzing down the wide expanse of highway, Scooter told us of his plans. "Right before you guys came out of the airport, I got a call from Jermaine Dupri. He challenged me to a video game at the studio, NBA 2K8. You guys mind if we stop in for a bit?"

Justin piped up from the backseat. "Oh, I love that game! Can I play with you guys?"

Scooter looked at Justin in the rearview mirror. "Of course," he said with a wink and a smile. "But be prepared to lose."

It was game on for Justin. He wasn't one to pass up a friendly competition. As the downtown skyscrapers started appearing in front of us on the horizon, Scooter and Justin kept up the smack talk.

I loved how the two of them immediately hit it off. Scooter was silly and had a knack for making Justin laugh, especially when he broke out in his "surfer dude" voice. I was quiet, observing the two of them, still skeptical of the opportunity and where it would lead. I was focused on being a mother, staying grounded and not getting caught up in the whirlwind of what could very well be a lucrative career for Justin in the music industry. I couldn't afford to throw away my brain. I needed to observe without distraction.

By then, I didn't doubt that Scooter was successful and had accomplished some big things. I was just a mama bear who wasn't easily impressed. While I appreciate and respect talent and achievements, my priority was being Justin's mother. My job, first and foremost, was to protect and watch over him, to keep his best interests in mind at all times. So while I respected Scooter, I really didn't focus on who he knew or how well he was connected. I was on guard for the sake of my son. In the entertainment business, it's easy to get swept away in the fame, the flash, and the glamour—all the sexy things most people believe encompass the music world.

Right when we pulled up to the studio, a black Range Rover pulled up alongside us. When Justin saw who got out of the truck, he practically cannonballed out of the backseat. Dressed in a leather jacket and wearing designer shades, Usher looked cool and almost aloof as he swaggered past us into the studio.

"Hey, Usher," Justin called out, taking longer strides to catch up with one of his music heroes. "I'm a huge fan and I know your songs. Can I sing you one?"

Usher smiled and politely brushed us off. "Some other time, buddy. It's cold outside." We wouldn't see him until our next trip a few months later.

Scooter asked if I could wait in the lobby while he and Justin went inside the studio. Of course I could. But I'll be honest. Though I knew it wasn't personal, I was disappointed. I knew Scooter wanted to play it cool and not make a big deal out of Justin meeting Jermaine (I think he even may have introduced Justin as his nephew). But to some extent, it made me feel left out.

Here I was, a mother who had spent the last thirteen years single-handedly raising her son. It had been us against the world. And now we were in another country, facing some important decisions, and we were apart. I never liked being away from Justin, even now. I walked around the lobby while I waited, trying to keep myself distracted. There were plaques lining the wall showcasing platinum and gold records from artists like Mariah Carey and Destiny's Child. Pretty cool, I thought, but I still wasn't sold.

Later that day, Scooter took us to his friend's high-rise apartment, where we would stay for the week. The minute we walked into the posh pad on the thirty-second floor, I felt I had just been transported inside a luxury interior design magazine. The place was a stylish and sleek ultramodern bachelor pad. It boasted shiny hardwood floors, a white plush sheepskin at the foot of a candy apple red leather couch, floor-to-ceiling windows with stunning views of downtown, and Justin's all-time favorite, the biggest flat-screen TV he had ever seen. The bedrooms were stark white, almost blinding, and uncluttered, with little in them except for more flat-screen TVs and the most comfortable beds we'd ever slept in. It was official. Justin and I had died and gone to *MTV Cribs* heaven.

We had a blast just hanging out inside the apartment. We were fascinated by the unique decorative accents that adorned the place, like the box of dominoes with real diamonds and the alligator skull that Justin couldn't stop touching. We must have taken a hundred pictures just of the stunning apartment. Justin was wide-eyed the entire trip, breaking out in "Oh, cool, Mom," and "Check this out," every two minutes. Atlanta was nothing like Stratford. It was a fast-paced metropolis and made the small town where I grew up seem even smaller.

In between our meetings with different producers and singers, Scooter got a call one day from his dad who lived in Connecticut. He was on his way home and had a layover in Atlanta. Scooter hoped the four of us could meet at the airport before his dad's flight home.

Before we ever met in person, Scooter had talked about the importance of morals and family values and how from day one his parents instilled in him good character. But talking and living it out are two totally separate things. So I was looking forward to meeting with his dad to get a glimpse of Scooter's roots and to see the dynamic of their relationship in action. If Scooter was going to be Justin's manager and a significant influence in his life, I wanted to be sure he was a man of integrity. And what better way to find out than by meeting his father?

Ervin Braun, a dentist with a thriving practice, met us at the food court. I believe he had just come back from a wakeboarding trip. A tall, handsome man, he had an unmistakable presence, a self-assured but not arrogant ease. He was also remarkably down-to-earth, one of the nicest men I've ever met. At one point Scooter walked his dad over to a quiet hallway, away from the clamor of fifty simultaneous conversations and the bustle of fast-food joints, so Justin could sing for him. Ervin enjoyed the private performance.

Over deli sandwiches, I peppered Scooter's dad with questions, repeating my fears and concerns about Justin being in the entertainment industry. Throughout our entire meeting, he stressed that his son was trustworthy, had integrity, and would take great care of us. I know Ervin's assurance wasn't merely a sales pitch. Every word was sincere. I had pretty good gut instincts; I just knew it.

But I didn't just take Ervin's words at face value; I read between the lines. I watched him interact with his son. The love between father and son was evident, as was a mutual respect and like-mindedness. Their relationship made quite an impression on me. I knew Scooter came from a good family, and meeting Ervin helped me eventually seal the deal.

We left Atlanta without making any official commitments. Justin was still in school, and I didn't plan to take him out before the year was over. While I wasn't ready to rush into anything, Justin was locked and loaded. If it were up to him, we would have signed on the dotted line before we headed back to Canada. I told Scooter we'd be in touch to discuss what it would look like if we did decide to move forward with him as Justin's manager.

I was honest with my son, doing my best to walk the thin line of encouraging him while still doling out a healthy medicinal dose of reality. "I know all of this is amazing, an unbelievable opportunity," I told him. "But don't get your hopes up. I haven't made a decision yet." I didn't want to be Debbie Downer, but truth was, I still hadn't come to a definite conclusion. Yes, I had confirmation by way of the answers to my two biggest questions, but I was still wrestling with the decision. There was so much at stake, and it wasn't about me. This was about Justin, my only child. I needed time and absolute peace before I took the leap and uprooted our lives to another country.

Two or three weeks after our trip to Atlanta, I made the decision. Between the natural progression of my relentless prayers, the confirmation of my two fleeces, the peace that settled my spirit, Scooter's diligence, and Justin's passionate drive, the answer was clear. I called Scooter—we were going to take the leap and move to Atlanta. He started drawing up the contracts.

I was thrilled for Justin, excited to see how this new chapter in his life would unfold page by page. Of course, I still had my concerns about the unpredictability of the music industry and the harsh reality of what can happen to young artists. As a mother those worries—and frankly, worry in general—can entice me. Once the wheels were set in motion after Scooter officially became Justin's manager, they spun so fast it was dizzying. It was time to plan our move to the United States.

I had plenty of serious talks with Justin during this time. I lavished him with encouragement and love, always quick to tell him how proud I was. But at the same time, I didn't want him to have a false sense of himself. I never tired of reminding him where his gifts came from and how he found himself surrounded by incredible opportunities. As a mother, I needed to make sure I instilled in him a balanced perspective, a solid understanding of the backdrop of his rising popularity and future career.

I remembered the verse, "A gift opens doors for the one who gives it and brings him into the presence of great people" (Prov. 18:16). So many times, in different ways, I warned Justin, "You can take credit for being disciplined and working hard to hone your talents, but you can't take credit for being naturally good at them. God gave you these gifts. And the only reason you're in this position is because of Him."

Though I never shoved my faith down Justin's throat, I gave him a strong foundation. I equipped him with certain beliefs and values knowing full well he would have to make the choice how to live his life and what paths he would follow. It will always be his choice.

Though Justin was still in school and I didn't plan on taking him out until the year was over, he was beside himself. Meanwhile, life continued its steady pace back in Stratford. I worked, Justin went to school, and we posted videos online. That was pretty much it.

Scooter and I worked together to build up Justin's YouTube following. We stayed up endless nights monitoring the channel, posting videos, and watching his popularity climb. Though we piqued the interest of a few record labels, nobody bit until Scooter brought in Usher and Justin Timberlake. It was an honor just to be considered by both camps. Though we ultimately decided to work with Usher, I feel that we wouldn't have lost either way.

I remember the trip to see Usher in February of 2008. Justin was stoked to meet one of his idols. I admit, I was pretty excited myself. I grew up listening to his music and admired him. The trip was short but eventful. Usher met us at what looked like a dance studio. A mirror lined one wall and chairs were scattered about. Justin did his thing, singing songs like "I'll Be" by Edwin McCain and even Usher's "U Got It Bad." In the middle of a riff in the latter song, Justin playfully asked Usher, "You gonna sing with me or what?" and kept right on crooning. He wasn't nervous. Not one bit. A natural performer, Justin never gets nervous.

Justin and Usher hit it off. The two of them shared a competitive streak. Usher's favorite game was Connect Four, and Justin mentioned he hadn't played in a while. At one or two in the morning, hours before we were scheduled to fly back to Canada, Usher had a Connect Four game and a Rubik's Cube dropped off for Justin. We were touched by the sweet gesture. And Justin was itching to practice so he could play Usher one day and beat him.

When I shared with my parents the news about moving to Atlanta after the school year, they were excited. They recognized the fact that Justin was presented with an opportunity for greatness. Like any grandparents would be, though, they were also heartbroken that their grandson would be eight hundred miles away. Bruce was crushed. He and Justin shared a special bond, one that Justin couldn't replicate with another human being, not even his grandmother or me.

I had never seen Bruce shed a tear until Justin performed in the Stratford Star contest. Something about Justin evoked deep emotion. When we told him and my mom about our decision to move, Bruce was a blubbering mess. He was going to miss his little boy. The two of them were a team. Every Friday night, he and Justin would watch the local hockey game at the Allman Arena. Bruce also accompanied me to every one of Justin's hockey games and even took him to most of his practices.

As apprehensive as I continued to be about the potential pitfalls and temptations that colored the entertainment world, I knew there would be more of a safety net around my son in Atlanta than there would have been in high school back home. Without being around Justin 24-7 in Stratford, known on the streets as the "meth capital" of Canada, I wouldn't know what kind of trouble he could get into, and believe me, even though it was a small city, there was a lot of trouble around.

From the start, Scooter and I were careful to choose the right people to work with and be around Justin. Though we may not agree on everything and may hold different philosophies, Scooter and I have the same commitment to protecting Justin. We made a conscious decision not to surround him with "yes" men or women. We wanted people on his team who would challenge his character and encourage his integrity. So while the move made me anxious for various reasons, I felt confident about my son's well-being. I knew Scooter and I would always have our fingers on the pulse of Justin's daily comings and goings.

Reality has a way of doing a disappearing act when you're caught up in the upheaval of a major life change. Emotions get sidelined as lengthy to-do lists take precedence. But once the cyclonic fury of tasks—like downsizing your life of thirty-three years into a few suitcases, gathering together medical records and school transcripts, and working out the logistics of moving to another country—dies down to a manageable lull, it happens. Reality pops in like a distant cousin coming for a surprise visit. I had to face the inevitable of saying goodbye to the comforts of the familiar and greeting the uncertainty of the new.

The last month before I vacated my apartment was full of tears. Lots of tears. The days merged into one another as I mourned the loss of the familiar place where I had been born and raised. I took long drives on miles of empty roads alongside picturesque farms on the outskirts of the city. I drove through the charming streets of downtown Stratford, past the library where Justin and I would pore over books like *Clifford the Big Red Dog* and the Arthur series. I drove past old neighborhoods, reminiscing to myself about my best friends on the block and throwing penny carnivals.

I was leaving behind places and things that provided comfort, that gave me joy, that made me laugh, that offered safety. Everything I had ever known and grown to love about Stratford—from the beautiful river where my son and I admired graceful swans and fed quacking ducks to the theater stage I had performed on and called my second home to homey diners and cafés where my best friends and I would spend hours talking—would be mere memories, eight hundred miles away from my new hometown of Atlanta, Georgia. (Not to mention, there was no Tim Hortons in Atlanta! I had drunk Tim Hortons coffee every day of my adult life! What was I going to do?)

As soon as I gave my landlord notice, my mom swept in like an army general. She got the ball rolling and began the task of getting rid of my stuff. We couldn't take much to Atlanta—only whatever could fit in a suitcase or two. Room by room, corner by corner, piece by piece, most of my belongings and furniture started disappearing. My mom made quick decisions. This was sold. That was donated. This was thrown out. That was given to a friend. I was grateful for her support, but sometimes she moved at such a rapid pace I couldn't keep up.

There were moments I needed time. I needed space. I needed to process the fact that bits and pieces of my life, all that I had accumulated over the years, were making their way out of the apartment. In the time it takes to blink—at least that's how it felt—I found myself a week or two before the move, living in an apartment furnished only with a mattress in the middle of the living room. A handful of Justin's clothes were strewn in one corner, and a few outfits of mine hung in the closet. The apartment wasn't the only thing that was bare. I too felt empty. I cried. I didn't even know where I could find an extra blanket.

Before my apartment was stripped bare, I had a lot of cleaning to do. I'll never forget one time when I walked around holding an overstuffed trash bag in one hand. I filled it with old, broken toys that Justin had stopped playing with years ago. Tears fell. Again. He wasn't a baby anymore. He wasn't even a little kid. Justin was growing up and literally going places, trekking into unknown territory, a strange landscape I didn't have a manual or GPS system to help navigate his way through. It seemed not but a day ago when Justin was banging on his high chair, playing the drums for the first time. Was it really over a decade later?

I would stand alone in the empty apartment on moving day, surrounded by the awful off-white walls that looked permanently dirty. As I gazed around the rooms—past the kitchen counter I could never get clean enough, the old appliances that had seen more than enough years, the nicks and scratches on the walls—my eyes landed on the floor of the hallway. I stared at it for a few minutes for no particular reason. The vinyl tiles always looked cracked. It was hard to tell simply by looking at it if the floor was dirty or purposely patterned that way. Though my heart ached from the roller coaster of memories that sped through my mind, I felt sure about one thing: I was definitely not going to miss this dingy apartment.

As my friend Scott, a lifesaver in those last few weeks, helped move some of the heavier things out to the garbage dump one day, I crumpled into his arms like a rag doll. I sobbed on his shoulder, feeling the unbearable weight of this new transition. Though a new chapter was about to be written, I felt my very life, the one I had built, slipping away from my fingers. When we walked out toward the end of the street, from the corner of my eye, I could see the local convenience store where Justin got slushies almost every day after school. Another round of tears fell, turning Scott's white T-shirt into a saline-soaked mess.

Scott took me, Justin, and one of Justin's best friends, Chaz, camping at Pinery Provincial Park a week before we left for Atlanta.

It helped to take some of the edge off our anxiety. For a few days, we hiked while we swatted away annoying mosquitoes in the afternoon humidity. We cooled off in the calm, clear waters of the lake and played on the wide sand dunes. Justin and Chaz spent hours building tiny teepee fires. At night, we huddled in our sleeping bags in a cozy tent, falling asleep under the moonlight to the sound of chirping crickets.

Every time I hear the songs "Better Together" by Jack Johnson and "1234" by Fiest, I think back on that trip. We listened to those two songs over and over on repeat. They remind me of how free we felt, enjoying the beauty of nature, singing silly campfire songs, and seemingly not having a care in the world. That was the point—fun. I wanted to give Justin one last impromptu trip. I wanted him to spend time with his best friend and not have to deal, at least for a little while, with the conflicting emotions I was sure he was wrestling.

As the countdown to moving got closer to the actual day, I threw Justin a huge going-away party on our friend Chad's farm. My son was surprised at how many people came to support him. From what I saw, it looked like every student from his junior high was there. Some played volleyball or rode quads, and others hung out by the long buffet table of chips and other unhealthy and greasy snacks that kids love. When the sun set, the teenagers gathered around a huge crackling bonfire and sang songs, led by Justin on his guitar. He even busted out solo performances, singing songs like "Cry Me a River" by Justin Timberlake. Toward the end of the night, fireworks lit up the sky in a colorful celebration.

My own going-away party was nowhere near as big or elaborate. I invited about fifty people I knew. Only nine showed up, including John's wife, Sue, and their daughter, Tasha. Though I was disappointed that so many people couldn't make it, we had a blast. It was my first time at a country-western bar. We tore up the dance floor, stomping our way through unfamiliar dance steps as Charlie Daniels and a fiddle blared through the speakers.

I even mustered up the courage, thanks to unrelenting peer pressure from my friends, to hop on the mechanical bull later that night.

I gripped the fake cowhide with my thighs with all my might as the bull violently bucked with so much force I could barely hold on. As the crowd hooted and hollered like only country-western fans could, I was finally thrown off and landed like a splash of splattered paint on the cushioned floor (I give myself props for not getting bucked off in the first fifteen seconds!).

The night before we left, Justin and I spent a few hours driving around town. It was our turn to reminiscence and say goodbye together. We didn't talk much but blasted the stereo as we always did. As the schools Justin attended, the skate park he frequented, and the parks we had explored faded from our view, we said goodbye.

Fifteen

Many people dream of starting over, though it's wishful thinking for most. Who wouldn't want a clean slate, an opportunity to meet new people who don't know who you are, the mistakes you've made, or your bad habits?

Moving to Atlanta marked my new beginning, and though I was grateful for the fresh start, I was in an emotional labyrinth—feeling homesick, eager for the new adventure, and apprehensive about what lay ahead.

I believed in Justin with all my heart and was excited for his new future. I knew without a doubt how talented he was and how badly he wanted this. I just didn't know what to expect, especially coming from a small town in Canada. The demographic differences alone were overwhelming. Stratford has a population of thirty thousand people and one of the lowest crime rates in all of Canada. Atlanta is one of the most dangerous cities in the United States, with a crime rate five times the national average. Over five million people call the Atlanta metropolitan area home. That's a big difference.

Scooter warned us he would be gone the first week after our move. He didn't mean for it to happen; it was just bad timing. The day we arrived in Atlanta was like a fog. Scooter dropped us off at a hotel in Buckhead, gave us three hundred bucks for the week, and took off on a business trip. I won't sugarcoat it. It was a rough week.

The area where we stayed was breathtaking. The hotel was nestled in one of the most expensive communities in Atlanta. We were surrounded by luscious landscaping and surprisingly clean streets flanked by architecturally stunning buildings, some of them housing high fashion boutiques that were too pricey to even window-shop. It was glitzy, but hard to enjoy. Though I appreciated Scooter's generosity, everything was so expensive that we couldn't do much venturing out. I certainly wasn't going to pay twenty bucks for a hamburger or seventy-five dollars a ticket to see a show. Besides, Justin and I were in an unfamiliar area. I didn't feel safe exploring on our own.

The stress of moving, being alone, and not knowing a soul took a toll on me not long after we arrived. Though I was incredibly anxious about the traumatic move, I was thankful that my anxiety and depression weren't as bad as they had once been. In fact, a few months before the move, with the help of my doctors, I completely weaned myself off the daily medication.

Still, that first week I was overwhelmed. My head exploded in a migraine. Looking back, I feel terrible for Justin. The pain was so debilitating, I couldn't do much aside from lay in bed all day. My poor son went stir crazy in our small hotel room. We fought a lot. It was almost impossible not to.

Kenny Hamilton, Scooter's good friend who would end up being one of Justin's bodyguards, showed up at our hotel room one day. He was a godsend and rescued my son. He took Justin out a few times that week while I nursed my migraine, huddled under hotel sheets trying not to move. I'll never forget Kenny's kindness that week—and to this day.

A week later, Scooter was back and we spent a few nights at his girlfriend's parents' house. Finally it was time to go home—our new home tucked away in a quiet community in the middle of the city. The three-story townhouse was beautiful. Just walking through the front doors helped to settle my nerves. The place was empty. Everything was brand-new and clean, nothing at all like my old apartment. *Hello, new home.*

The three of us drove to a furniture store where Scooter footed the bill for an array of "previously enjoyed" couches, tables, and bedroom sets. We also took a trip to Target and loaded up two carts with every household item imaginable—toilet paper, dishes, towels, pots, pans, sheets, clocks, and toiletries. Our final stop was a grocery store. I've never bought so much food in my life (thanks, Scooter!). We stocked our fridge and pantry with condiments, cereal, pasta, fruits, vegetables, snacks, soda, and juices. As a single mother who had spent the last thirteen years either on government assistance or counting pennies, I felt like we had hit the lottery. Setting up house was really fun. Starting over and having all new things was exciting and freeing.

Still, leaving everything and everyone we knew was really hard on me because we didn't know anyone outside of Scooter and Kenny. We didn't have a church. We didn't have a network of support. Even the friends I had back home seemed to be too busy to connect. I missed home so much it physically hurt. I cried for six months.

My plan was to find a church right away. I was sure I'd find one in no time—with Atlanta being located in the Bible Belt, there was one on practically every corner. I'd get plugged in, join a small group, get to know some people, go out for coffee or dinner with my new friends, and resume a supportive social network. No such luck. I struggled to find a church I could call home.

I tried. I church-hopped multiple services on Sundays. I went to megachurches, small churches, churches with dynamic worship, churches involved in social outreach. They all had positive features, but I didn't connect with any one in particular for at least six months in Atlanta. I'd sit in a pew Sunday after Sunday, enjoying good music and a good sermon. As I stared at the people around me, hugging each other hello, asking about so-and-so's kids and what they're doing for lunch and could they make something for the potluck next week, I wanted to disappear into the cushioned seats.

The failure to get plugged in somewhere had an effect on my faith. In some ways I felt like God abandoned me. I couldn't feel His presence. It was one of my darkest spiritual hours. I developed phobias and fears I'd never had before. I was afraid of flying, for one. For about eight months after the move, anytime I boarded a plane, I'd plant myself in the seat and dig my nails into the armrests. I'd close my eyes so tight they would hurt. Mere seconds away from hyperventilating, I'd repeatedly whisper, "Please don't let me die. Please don't let me die." If Justin wanted to go to the amusement park, I refused to ride the roller coasters or any tall waterslides because I was convinced I would die, which was so out of character for me. Almost every night for weeks I was plagued with dreams about falling off a bridge and crashing to my death on rocks in shallow water.

I tried to encourage myself, determined not to let these feelings of being abandoned by God destroy my beliefs. I prayed. Oh, how I prayed. I read my Bible more than usual, poring over its words as well as listening to an audio version. But I still couldn't escape the gnawing feelings of fear and anxiety that were eating through my peace like termites.

I wrestled with God in the middle of the night, when Justin was sound asleep in his bed. I wrestled with God when the sun was slowly creeping up over the horizon, shedding its hazy orange glow over early morning joggers. I wrestled with God while I was stuck in traffic on Atlanta's congested highways. "Where are You, God?" I would cry out. "Are You mad at me? Did I hear You wrong about moving here? Why do I feel like You are rejecting me?"

My heart broke as the tears fell. But however slighted or left behind I felt, I was determined not to let go of Him, even if I was only barely holding on to a thread of faith. I clung to God with all my might, against all odds. I was familiar with these dark nights of the soul and knew that despite my feelings, I had to hold on . . . a little longer . . . and maybe even a little longer yet.

I had moments of relief when I was encouraged by a message, an old friend's heartfelt prayer, or feeling the familiar presence of God I hadn't experienced in a while. Over time, inch by inch, the darkness began to lift. The unmanageable weight of panic started to slip off my shoulders. My heart eased its way into more of a settling calm. And all of the fears and phobias that I had suddenly developed vanished.

I think my spiritual and emotional unrest was the result of the extreme change. I had to dig deep with God during this time. It challenged me to cope with my faith on my own, outside of depending on someone else. Extreme change would become my new normal as we entered the fast-paced life of nonstop travel and spending time in a different hotel room every night.

Things were happening so big and so fast for Justin. Between watching him record and traveling with him doing radio promos all over the country, I was responsible for signing contracts that could affect a large portion of Justin's life. Pages and pages of legal jargon were being presented to me each day, and even though I had an attorney who helped walk me through each paragraph, it was still a daunting task. At the end of the day, I was Justin's mother. I was accountable for the repercussions that could come from any document I signed or deal I authorized.

There were times fear inched its way into my heart. I was afraid of making a mistake. I felt so much pressure. What if I signed something that could steer Justin in the wrong direction? Or chained him to an obligation that would only hurt him in the long run? Or put him in the path of unhealthy, long-term relationships?

But I couldn't allow those questions and fears to cripple my confidence. I remembered who brought us to this place, who aligned every detail so I would know our move was God-ordained. God wouldn't have put me in this situation to make me fail or fall. I began to listen to my instincts and follow the peace in my heart. I'm sure I made mistakes along the way, but what parent doesn't?

Eventually I did find a church I could call home. I also met a man there on my first visit whom I half-jokingly refer to as my angel. Brandon was visiting from Maryland when I met him. After we connected at the persuasion of the pastor, we instantly bonded. Brandon became our travel pastor, hitting the road with Justin and his team for a few years. Justin needed a mentor, and while Scooter was definitely a great influence, he could only do so much. Scooter always ran at full steam doing the million things that were required to manage Justin's exploding career, so my son needed someone who could be fully devoted to his character, someone who could pray with and help lead him. Brandon was the guy. Only in his early twenties, he meshed well with Justin. They loved to rap and would spend hours writing songs together. Brandon recently got married and started a new life, leaving behind his role as Justin's pastor and being on the road with him. But I'll always be grateful for the way he invested in my son during that time period.

The rest of the story is history. Most of you know it well: The platinum-selling albums. The multiple Billboard hits. The worldwide number-one singles. The Grammy Awards. The American Music Awards. The world tours. The fans. The absolutely amazing fans.

I'm so proud of Justin. I'm in awe of how far he has come and how tirelessly he works to entertain his fans. One thing I've always admired about my son is his ability to switch from Justin Bieber the performer to Justin Bieber the normal teenager. From the start he didn't allow the cameras, the hype, the screaming fans, the glitz, or the glamour to strip him of his roots.

It reminds me of the time he sang a special number during a concert early in his career. I was fascinated by how calm, cool, and collected Justin was. It was probably the first moment I knew beyond a shadow of a doubt that he was made for this. That he was born to perform.

This was Justin's first big performance. By this time he had done small shows and appearances during his radio promo tour all over the country, but nothing at all like this. This was the big leagues.

This was his breakout moment. Justin had a giant online following at this point—nothing close to what he has now, of course—and the publicity for the major event was off the hook. Thousands of concertgoers filled the massive stadium. Pops of lights flashed. The thunderous roar of screaming girls made it impossible to even think.

I was nervous for my son, pacing anxiously around backstage in the company of Scooter and Ryan (Justin's road manager/stylist who traveled with us everywhere). I had a gnawing feeling in the pit of my stomach. I was sure Justin would spend the last moments before he was due to perform having some quiet time alone, needing to rehearse and focus. I wanted to give Justin a pep talk, to remind him to relax and that he'd do great. Because that was what he needed, right? Encouragement from his mama to ease his nerves?

Ready to wrap my arms around him in a warm hug just moments before his performance, I couldn't believe what I saw when I found him backstage. He was huddled over a laptop furiously playing a typing game he was obsessed with at the time. Didn't he know he had three minutes before he had to take the stage? Didn't he know he was about to sing in front of thousands of screaming fans?

"Justin," I said sharply. "You have three minutes. Get off that stupid game!"

Not even bothering to look up, he remained engrossed in his computer, brushing me off as if I had just asked him to clean his room. "Wait. Just wait, Mom, I'm almost done. I'm about to beat my high score!"

What did he just say? Are you kidding me? I was dumbfounded. He wasn't the least bit concerned that time was ticking, that the pressure was on. This was a big deal.

"Justin," I snapped. "Get off the computer!"

"Hang on, Mom, just hang on. Let me finish this."

And just in the nick of time, less than a minute before he was due onstage and only seconds away from me physically prying the computer out of his fingers, Justin slammed the lid shut. Looking at me with a huge grin, he jumped out of his seat and said, "Done!" He grabbed a nearby microphone and made a mad dash toward the stage. I heard Justin shout out without missing a beat, "How's it going, New York?" to the sound of a shrieking crowd.

Even as the pressure grew, he remained a typical teenager. I'll never forget what happened after one of his shows early on. We rushed out of the arena, having only thirty short minutes to make it to Justin's next radio appearance. Security officers surrounded us as we had to politely battle our way through the few hundred girls who were waiting outside for Justin. Our car seemed like it was a mile away, and I felt stuck in the midst of screaming teenagers and multiple pairs of outstretched arms that tried to reach out for Justin. Someone finally threw open the car door, and we hurried inside. I slammed the door shut and breathed a sigh of relief.

Driving off posed a challenge. The girls wouldn't let us through. The mob required additional reinforcements of security officers to clear a path so we could drive out of the parking lot without running someone over. No amount of personnel could tame the crowd. The driver slowly inched his way onto the side street as girls pounded on the window chanting Justin's name and screaming, "I love you, Justin!" The noise was deafening. The girls slammed on the car so hard, it felt like twenty-pound barbells were dropping out of the sky like rain. The car rocked back and forth from the seismic activity.

I took in the moment, amused and shocked by the madness. *How the heck did we get here?* I wondered. *How did this happen?* Justin, however, was oblivious to the entire chaotic scene. He was talking to his grandmother on his cell phone the entire time, chatting away as nonchalant as ever. "How are you, Grandma?" he asked. "How was your day?" He wasn't Justin Bieber, pop star. He was Justin, grandson.

Despite how his career has exploded, Justin has always remained determined not to forget his roots. And I've done the same.

Sixteen

They were just like me.

And I was just like them.

In a narrow hallway lined with young women clad in black T-shirts and jeans, I stood among them not just as a curious visitor but also as a knowing survivor. As a person who'd felt similar pain.

I was on a tour of the Los Angeles campus of the Dream Center, a volunteer organization that meets the physical and spiritual needs of the community through nearly three hundred programs including a local and a mobile food bank, a mobile medical clinic, a rehab center for recovering addicts, and even a shelter for sex trafficking victims. Think of any need in the Los Angeles area, and the Dream Center probably has a program to fill it. Pastor Matthew Barnett, the founder of the organization and now a good friend of mine, calls it a twenty-four-hour spiritual hospital. To those who go there, it's a lifeline.

A few days earlier, I had visited Pastor Matthew's church. Lesley, one of my best friends, attends there and is involved in a few of their many outreach programs. She had told me great things about the Dream Center and the church, and I was curious to visit.

Matthew spoke that day. I'll never forget what he said: "It's great to gather together for church on Sunday, but real church starts Monday morning." His message touched on some of the work that was being done through the Dream Center. I was intrigued and couldn't wait for Lesley to show me around the nine-acre campus after church. I wanted to get a taste of what the headquarters of such an incredibly bighearted and mission-oriented organization looks like.

As we drove, Lesley talked about the various programs. I didn't say much but soaked in the experience. My eyes were drawn to a group of women wearing the same clothes and walking in unison. They looked like an army battalion, moving with purpose and carrying themselves with pride. Lesley told me they were part of the women's program. "They're here for a second chance," she said. I was deeply touched, moved by their courage to step out and be a part of the Dream Center ministry.

Tears streamed down my face as we continued to drive past large brick buildings with simple but neatly manicured lawns. "There's the food bank where they process over one million pounds of donated groceries a month." My mouth dropped. That's a lot of food. "And there's the teen unit, and over there is the men's unit. The next one down is the women's unit. There are over five hundred people living here at one time." Lesley also showed me the renovated ambulances that drove around impoverished neighborhoods providing free medical care. We ended our drive passing by a diner that had servers, menus, and a wide selection of delicious food—all for free.

Seeing firsthand this amazingly orchestrated mission at work left me speechless. That night I tweeted, "Matthew Barnett is my new hero. He is truly the hands and feet of Jesus." He tweeted back, "If you ever want a tour, let me know."

One morning not long after, Matthew drove me around the campus showing me every facet of this incredible ministry. He had also arranged for a handful of men, women, and teens from different programs to share with me why they were at the Dream Center and how their lives had changed.

When we arrived at the women's division, my heart was full of anticipation. I stood in front of them and wondered what brought these women, some as young as nineteen, to a place of so desperately needing help. Matthew introduced three of them who would share their testimonies with me. I listened as they unfolded the tapestries of their lives—tattered, worn, and miraculously beautiful. Their stories were heartbreaking.

I heard a former porn actress tell how she ran away from home, got involved with drugs and the wrong crowd, and met a young man who convinced her she'd make a great escort. Her sexual escapades eventually led her to star in pornographic films. Unable to cope with reality, she numbed her pain with her meth addiction.

Another woman shared about her physically abusive relationship, how she overdosed on drugs and was left for dead in a coma, and the fifteen-year prison sentence she faced at the mere age of twenty.

I watched the last young woman fight back tears as she told a tale of abandonment. Her stepfather sexually abused her repeatedly. While on a family vacation in Los Angeles, he beat her almost to the point of death. She woke up in a hospital and was told by a police officer that her parents had left her. She became a ward of the state, bouncing from foster home to foster home until she was lost in the system. Using drugs was an escape from being unwanted; selling them bought her escape.

Hearing their stories, I felt a familiar blow to my gut. I could relate. I wanted these young women to know I understood both their pain and their triumph. So when they thanked me for allowing them to share a piece of their hearts with me, I asked if they were willing to hear my story. They agreed.

Earlier, Matthew had simply introduced me as Pattie, one of his friends taking a tour of the Dream Center. He didn't mention who my son is. I shared with these precious women the trauma of the day my dad walked out. I told them about how sexual abuse had left me vulnerable and afraid over the years. About how pain and emptiness drove me to drink, abuse drugs, and attempt suicide. I walked them through finding myself pregnant and alone at eighteen, admitting that I hadn't been ready to be a mom.

But I didn't stop there. I also told them about the grace in my story. About second (and third and fourth) chances. I wanted to remind them to keep going, to not give up, to keep believing their lives could stay turned around, not just for a little while but for the rest of their lives. Only when I came to the end of this story of a broken heart made whole, of a life restored, and of love found did I reveal one last piece of the puzzle. "And now here I stand before you as Justin Bieber's mom," I said with a grin.

The crowd of young women gasped. Some of them were even crying. They were astonished that the roads we had traveled were so similar and that we had something in common—we all found hope. We didn't want to spend the rest of our lives muddling through the murky, subterranean parts of our journey. Though we had certainly not arrived yet, we had found our way up.

Don't mistake their moved emotions as coming from excitement simply because I am the mother of a world-renowned pop star. Don't think for one minute that they were inspired only because of who I was. Understand this: it didn't have much to do with me. It was about seeing the evidence that things can change for the better, that "all things work together for the good of those who love God" (Rom. 8:28). They knew this, of course, based on their personal experiences. But my story offered further proof that you don't have to stay stuck in abuse, in addiction, in despair.

Though I have experienced pain, shame, fear, and abandonment, I have also experienced hope, promise, peace, and joy. I am overwhelmed at how God has lavished me with His love and His grace. How in spite of my past, my mistakes, and even my unfaithfulness, I have intimately experienced the goodness of His mercy. I love the verse in Psalms that says, "The LORD is close to the brokenhearted;

he rescues those whose spirits are crushed" (34:18 NLT). It's my testament. I wouldn't trade my pain away, for I know how deep my faith has grown as a result.

As Justin's career took off, I continued my healing journey. I had begun to face my demons and my past, unearthing deep wounds. It's an ongoing process. As I continued to struggle with anxiety and depression, they were indicators I had more healing to do.

I confess my healing has been—and continues to be—a long process. I don't make any claims that I've arrived at the final destination of emotional wholeness, but I am so much further than I ever imagined I could be. I am so much freer, full of life and peace in so many areas in my life.

When I began my journey of healing—of seeking out the broken places shattered by rejection, abandonment, and sexual abuse—I never realized how many layers of pain I would have to work through. And I never knew how hard it would be.

At times I thought I was going to break under the pressure. I would remind myself of the Scripture that shares how God "will not crush the weakest reed or put out a flickering candle" (Isa. 42:3 NLT). It told me that God understood my brokenness and would be gentle with me. He wouldn't be impatient when I didn't get it together immediately. He wouldn't push me past my breaking point. He wouldn't stretch me further than my capacity. He would take His time with me, not rushing the healing process.

My healing has taken so long, perhaps, because of the core lies I had believed since I was a little girl. Those untruths that shaped me in harmful ways were communicated to me by circumstances, people in my life, and even myself. It's taken me years to not only identify them but also replace them with truth. That was a challenge. Even though I knew certain things were true, they didn't always connect with the deepest part of me. Knowing something in your head and believing it in your heart are two different things. Once I was able to really grasp and embrace certain truths (many of which are found in Scripture), I was finally able to combat the lies and reclaim my identity.

For instance, I used to believe the lie that I was unlovable; now I know the truth that I am loved (Rom. 8:39). I used to believe I was full of shame; now I know I am forgiven (Rom. 8:1). I used to believe I was worthless; now I know I am valuable (Ps. 139:14). I used to believe there was no point to my existence; now I know the future is full of hope (Jer. 29:11). I used to feel rejected; now I know I am a daughter of God and my Father looks at me with eyes of approval (Zeph. 3:17). I used to believe I was a mistake; now I know I'm chosen (1 Pet. 2:9).

Whenever I felt depressed or anxious, I hammered these truths into me (I still do when I need to). I didn't allow myself to get caught up in old feelings that only served to reinforce emotional damage. I focused on hope. I focused on healing. I focused on truth. The truth really does set you free.

My healing from the sexual abuse I'd suffered over the years needed to take place on multiple levels. It wasn't just a matter of dealing with the actual acts that caused me emotional damage. I also had to deal with what happened to me as a result. The abuse had created in me shame, anxiety, and fear. It had also skewed my view of love and sex. I believe so much of my brokenness stemmed from the fact that I didn't value or respect my sexuality.

After I lost my virginity, nothing about my sexuality seemed sacred to me. Having sex never felt wrong; it was part of my lifestyle. Something I did. Something I was expected to do. But when I was twenty-one, I started to feel like that part of my life was being challenged.

As a Christian, I knew sex was supposed to be reserved for marriage. But a few years after I gave my life to God, I was still struggling in that area. At that time a youth pastor invited me to a True Love Waits conference. The timing was perfect. I had no idea how to redeem or purify my sexuality. Frankly, I didn't think it was possible. As I listened to the message, my stomach was in knots. The more I heard the speaker talk about his tainted sexual past and how he reclaimed that part of his life, the more I so desperately wanted my own purity restored.

Even before the speaker had uttered the last word of his message, I realized this was my opportunity. This was my time. This was my way of taking back the part of my life that had been mutilated and destroyed. After the service, I signed a pledge—with my friend Kevin signing as a witness—not to have sex before I was married. My hand shook as I penned my name. Pattie Mallette—the girl who knew about sex at the same age she played with Cabbage Patch dolls. The girl who could finally have restored what had been so painfully broken.

I've never looked back. Yes, it's really hard. The temptation has been great at times. But I made a vow to God, something I take very seriously. It may seem prudish or old-fashioned in this day and age, but I've committed to honoring God by saving myself for marriage. I have no intention of reneging on that promise. (And yes, at the time of this writing, I'm still single.)

As I sought healing from my sexual abuse, my counselors guided me down a winding road of challenges. It started with a decision. I had to first admit my victimization and second refuse to be a victim. Yes, I was abused; no, I'm not going to live the rest of my life feeling sorry for myself. Healing would never fully find its way into my heart without me giving up a victim mentality. This didn't mean, however, I didn't mourn my pain. I had to love myself enough to grieve what I needed to grieve. I had to value myself enough to sift through the emotional wounds but not stay there.

I also would never be emotionally whole without learning to forgive others and, most importantly, myself. When I recently read the diary I had written during my teen years, I cringed. Drinking and smoking this much on that night. Getting wasted at a family get-together. Calling my mom every name in the book. A myriad of emotions surfaced.

I shook my head in disbelief. I was ashamed and embarrassed of the person I once was, someone so different from who I am today. I dropped the book on the floor, not wanting to ever pick it back up. I was even tempted to burn it. To remove it from existence.

Suddenly, I remembered the words, *Those who are hardest to love need it the most.*

I love that statement. I say it all the time to remind myself to handle certain people with care. I say it to my parents. I say it to my friends. I say it to Justin. Now I couldn't get the saying out of my mind. Then the thought came to me, *You apply this statement to everyone in your life, so why can't you accept it for yourself? Why can't you love you?* The truth was shocking. It wasn't the adult Pattie I didn't love. It was the teenage Pattie. I couldn't stand the hardened, rebellious, defiant teenager I used to be.

Days later, I revisited my thoughts with a counselor. I was finally able to sift through the discomfort. Faced head-on with the question and working through it with someone I trusted, I had an awakening. I started releasing the hatred I had for myself as a teenager, for the terrible decisions I had made, for the stupid things I had said and done.

I started to remember how my previous therapists had tried to get me to look in a mirror and say, "I love you." It was almost impossible. I tried it once or twice, but I hated it. It made me feel weird, strange. Even like an imposter. But if I don't love myself, how can I love others? And if I can't receive love, how can I give love? All the commandments can be summed up into two: "Love the Lord your God with all your heart, with all your soul, and with all your mind," and "Love your neighbor as you love yourself" (see Matt. 22:36–40). I can't love others if I don't love myself, so I'm learning how to love myself.

I wasn't the only person I needed to forgive. There were a lot of people in my life to whom I needed to extend the same grace—my dad, my mom, my abusers, Jeremy. Sometimes it felt never-ending. As I continued the healing process, I started realizing that forgiveness is not a one-shot deal. Simply saying "I forgive you" doesn't take away the pain, the hurt, or the injustice that was done. I had to continually live from a place of forgiving. Sometimes daily, sometimes even hourly.

There were times it seemed impossible. During my moments of struggle, I had to ask God for help. I figured if He was willing to send His only Son to die on a cross so I could be forgiven, surely He would be willing to help me forgive others. Though it didn't always happen instantaneously, I've found myself able to forgive through His grace alone. (I've also prayed for help when I needed to love others or be patient but didn't have the tools to do so.)

I love the saying, "Unforgiveness is like drinking poison and waiting for the other person to die." The fact was, if I didn't reach out and forgive, I'd be the one ultimately hurt. I would be held hostage by bitterness. My unforgiveness could even extend outward; it could affect me not just emotionally but in many areas such as my relationships or even physical health. Several medical studies have linked unforgiveness with sickness, disease, and depression.

One definition of forgiving is letting go of your right to get even. It doesn't mean the injustice was okay. While I didn't have a choice in how I was hurt or broken, I had a choice to forgive. I had a choice to let the pain define me or to heal from its wounds. I made the choice to heal. I made the choice to move on without those wounds crippling my journey. I made the choice to live. To *really* live. It has not been easy, but it has been worth it.

As I continue to focus on becoming emotionally whole, I'm excited to see what's in store. This certainly isn't the end of my story. It's only the beginning.

There's more to me than just being the mother of Justin Bieber. For the last eighteen years, I have dedicated my heart and soul to raising my son the best way I know how. Writing this book not only has been healing but is the first step into a new chapter of my life. I'm launching into my own destiny. A part of that means defining myself apart from my son as he transitions to adulthood (I'm sure any mom can relate). It also means further defining and expanding my purpose and my mission in life.

The amazing platform God has given my son has also opened doors for me to share my story, just like I did with the women at the Dream Center. I recently had the opportunity to visit the Bethesda Centre and talk to the girls there.

Though much of the building had been renovated and the rooms were rearranged, I felt a rush of memories. I could imagine myself as a scared teenager, trying to sort through a million questions and tame a flurry of overpowering emotions. Though I was the mom of an almost (at the time) eighteen-year-old son, I felt the anxiety of being pregnant as if it were yesterday. I felt the worry. The wonder. The pain.

As some of the staff showed me around the facility, we made a pit stop at a classroom where six girls who were either pregnant or new teen moms sat around a table. I smiled at their sweet faces. They looked so young and some of them so tired. I knew exactly what they must have been feeling in that moment—whether they were scared of the impending pain of giving birth, exhausted from lack of sleep from taking care of a newborn, or wondering what would happen to them after their time at Bethesda was over and they had to create a new life on their own.

The girls talked loudly and giggled nonstop, bombarding me with all kinds of questions about (who else?) Justin, like if he still had a girlfriend and what it's like being the mom of a famous pop star. It wasn't long, however, before their cute probing became more serious. The silly questions turned into honest statements that unmasked emotions and exposed insecurities.

I noticed one of the especially feisty girls had grown unusually quiet. Then she lowered her head and timidly lifted up her hand. I nodded toward her and she began to speak, tears cascading down her face.

"I feel like I have nothing to offer my baby," she sobbed. My heart broke as she continued to cry. I walked over to her and gave her a hug, holding her close for a few minutes. The other girls at the table nodded knowingly, brushing away compassionate tears from their own eyes. I imagine very few teen moms don't feel like they fall short.

I encouraged this precious girl with a heart of empathy. "I didn't feel like I had anything to offer either," I admitted. "I was young when I had Justin, and I had been through a lot of sexual abuse and hard stuff. It's part of the reason I'm here. I know how tough it is. I know exactly how you feel."

I looked her in the eye and continued. "What do you have to offer? Love. Love is so powerful. And you have yourself to offer. It's more than enough. If you take care of yourself, your life, and your heart, you can offer so much! Look at the kids who are born in third world countries. Their parents don't have much to give them except themselves and their hearts. And those children are some of the happiest in the world! Trust me, you have plenty to offer your baby."

I felt humbled by this girl's honesty and honored that I could share with her my experiences, my insecurities, and my doubts and show her through my life that she could be a good mother to her baby, no matter how old she was.

I will always have a special place in my heart for teen mothers. But it's not just teen moms who struggle or need to find hope. Whether you're a single mom, an addict, or a victim of abuse . . . whether you're on the verge of bankruptcy or the brink of divorce . . . whether you're in a dysfunctional family or the product of a broken home . . . whether you battle depression or struggle with anxiety . . . whether you live in fear or hide in shame . . . whether you've been abandoned, rejected, or ignored—there is hope.

It doesn't matter where you find yourself today—how broken, hurting, wounded, or ashamed you are. If God can help me find my way up, I promise, He can do the same for you.

Acknowledgments

To my son, Justin, my heart: I'm proud of you beyond words. You've brought so much joy into my life, and I've always known you were created for greatness. I'm grateful for you standing with me through this writing process. I know I haven't been able to travel with you as much lately. Know that I've missed you. (PS: I just had a burst of love for you.)

To my parents: Mom, you are and always have been a good mother. I'll always be grateful for your sacrifices for our family, from staying up nights when we were sick, to always being around, to cooking and cleaning every day and doing whatever it took to provide for our needs. Thank you, Mom. I love you. Bruce, thank you for being an amazing husband to my mom and loving her like you do. I know I wasn't always the easiest daughter, but you were always a good and faithful dad. (I never did grow up to be that boxer, but I did write a book!) You both are unbelievable grandparents.

To my siblings: Candie, I always looked up to you. You were a great big sister. Thanks for always listening to me and giving me advice. Chris, thanks for being a protective older brother and always scaring the bullies away. Sorry for always getting you in trouble when we were younger. To the other Chris, thanks for letting us call you Chuck and for being sweet and always making me laugh. Sally, I can't wait to meet you in heaven.

To Jeremy: I'm eternally grateful to you not only for giving me the greatest gift of my life, Justin, but also for becoming the man and father you are today. Though our relationship was rocky, I wouldn't take any of it back or change any of it because God has turned it all around for good and continues to do so. My intentions are not to hurt you. With that said, this is my side of the story that could not be possible without you. I love you. There will always be a special place in my heart for you.

To Lesley, my publicist and my assistant/manager/advisor/whatever-I-need-in-the-moment beast: You are amazing! Above all else, you are a really great friend. I treasure you.

To A. J., my co-writer, a wife, a mother to a baby girl, and an author: I honestly don't know how you do it. You work harder than any woman I know and somehow still manage to produce the gold. After countless hours together, I have gained a friend. We did it!

To Esther, my literary agent: Thank you for believing in me. You're the best at what you do.

To Dwight Baker and the team at Revell: Thank you for your hard work, your patience, your diligence, and your expertise. A special thanks to Jennifer and Twila for going the extra mile (specifically, 267 miles for Jen to drive to Canada).

To my abusers: I forgive you.

Pattie Mallette, known to most of the world as Justin Bieber's mom, is more than just the mother of a world-renowned pop sensation. Pattie walks a rarely traveled road parenting her son through the unpredictable journey of fame. As a young woman and a single mom, she fought hard to rise above her painful past of abuse, shame, and poverty. Pattie hopes to encourage troubled youth, struggling single moms, and the brokenhearted through her story. She continues to expand her outreach to young women and youth (including her nearly one million followers on Twitter) while overseeing the management of Justin and his team. Follow her on Twitter (@PattieMallette).

An accomplished writer, **A. J. Gregory** has collaborated with fascinating high-profile figures on nearly twenty books. She is also the author of *Silent Savior* and *Messy Faith*.